PureWool

Pure Wool

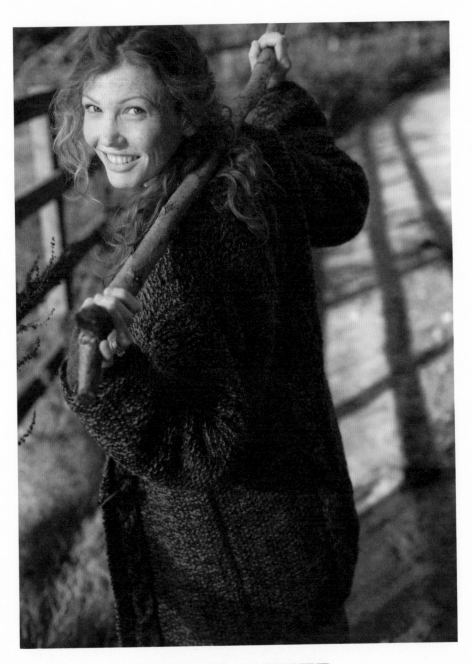

SUE BLACKER

STACKPOLE
BOOKS

A Quantum Book

Published by
STACKPOLE BOOKS
5067 Ritter Road
Mechanicsburg, PA 17055
www.stackpolebooks.com
Copyright © 2012 Quantum Publishing Ltd.

10 9 8 7 6 5 4 3 2 1

First edition

ISBN 978-0-8117-1103-6

This book is produced by
Quantum Publishing Ltd.
6 Blundell Street
London N7 9BH

QUMPURE

Cover design by Tessa J. Sweigert
Design: Louise Turpin
Managing Editor: Jennifer Eiss
Project Editor: Julie Brooke
Project Editor: Samantha Warrington
Assistant Editor: Jo Morley
Production Manager: Rohana Yusof
Publisher: Sarah Bloxham

Printed in China, by Hung Hing

The yarn requirements, knitted gauge and other
pattern information in this book are correct
when using the appropriate Blacker Yarns. If
you wish to substitute your own yarn you may
need more than specified in the patterns and
to use different needles. We strongly advise
you should always knit a gauge square before
starting to make a garment, especially when
using a substitute yarn. The information on
sheep breeds, including micron counts, is from a
variety of research but mainly from the practical
experience of The Natural Fibre Company and
may therefore differ from other sources.

Contents

Pure Wool Philosophy

The importance of using pure wool from specific breeds represents a passion and faith, as well as a philosophy. There is logic behind this passion and faith. You may be reading this because you feel the same way, but it is worth going over the basics, if only to help you to convince others!

The Campaign for Wool, and its patron, HRH The Prince of Wales, remind us that wool is:

- 100% natural: the fiber is not artificially made in oil refineries and chemical plants
- 100% renewable: sheep grow the wool every year for many years
- 100% sustainable: sheep live on land that cannot be managed and where crops and other animals cannot survive: high hills and fells, steep downlands, and, in some cases, even woodlands. For example, the White-faced Woodland sheep breed does not eat trees, unlike my Gotland sheep!

- 100% biodegradable: wool will rot back into the soil. However, this takes some time, and it is possible to store fleeces for three to four years. It can also be recycled
- warmer: it both insulates and permits the passage of air, so it can keep you warm and still be breathable
- safe: unlike cotton, igniting at 255° centigrade, and artificial fibers, variously 420-560°, wool does not catch fire until it reaches 600° centigrade
- hypoallergenic: it resists dirt and stains and the accompanying germs, so wool needs washing less than other fibers
- a part of our historic landscape. Imagine Britain without fields of sheep
- being used less, partly causing sheep numbers to have halved in twenty years

The logo of The Campaign for Wool (left) **and its patron** HRH Prince Charles (below left). **Baby Finley** tries a Blue-faced Leicester blanket.

Why wool for me?

Since learning to knit at around five years of age, and being involved with sheep since 1997, I have come on a long journey:

I discovered that all sheep owners believe their own sheep are the best, and they rarely have diseases or defects. I also discovered Gotland sheep. While they need a bit more care and are more suited to small flocks, they are determined to stay alive and healthy.

I found that sheep are intelligent with good memories (now the subject of research). One of my sheep, Jake, spent 30 minutes trying to break into the chicken house to get the grain, which suggests a degree of concentration—he was also working on the door catch, not any other part of the house. It's just that a set of teeth is not as good as a human hand!

I also discovered that wool is very rewarding, not just for the reasons above, but because it feels wonderful. There is a substance to wool which is hard to define. It is stimulating and rewarding to knit; calculating, experimenting, and watching the work grow. It is obvious to me, and now also to you I hope, that the arguments about and loveliness of natural wool should go hand-in-hand to sustain a future for both wool and sheep.

Somehow, I ended up with a breeding flock of Gotlands. I am starting to breed black Blue-faced Leicesters, and I run The Natural Fibre Company. This is not a lifestyle activity but a real business, with real people, products and results which are enthralling! The Natural Fibre Company is especially rewarding because its customers are so knowledgeable and interested in wool.

I also wanted to share what I have learnt. Finding the right yarn for a project is vital. The sheer versatility of wool and the possibilities of creating specific yarns for specific purposes are, perhaps, not fully appreciated. So we (the designers and knitters who made the patterns and samples, and everyone at The Natural Fibre Company) have tried to enable you to match the right fiber to the appropriate yarn and to a suitable design. We hope you enjoy it.

We hope this book will contribute to the history of farming, shepherding, industrial development, and textile design in Britain, and bring some of this back to its roots in local provenance, quality and values.

Susan Black

Sue farms Gotland sheep and wants everyone to enjoy pure wool.

pure wool basics

From farm to yarn

Sheep have been domesticated for 8,000 years, probably originating in the Middle East, then spreading around the Mediterranean and across Europe and Asia, reaching the UK 6,000 years ago.

The first sheep were small, multicolored animals. Over the centuries they have been bred to give more meat and wool.

By 3,900 years ago, the British were spinning wool and weaving cloth. Exports to Europe probably started 1,300 years ago, and by the early twelfth century, sheep and wool were central to the British economy. Innovations to speed up production were an important part of the Industrial Revolution in the eighteenth century.

The earliest known knitting—socks dated 1,500 years ago—are not truly knitting, but "nalbinding,"

a looped and knotted stitching made with a needle.

Examples of thirteenth-century knitted work have been found in Spain, but it was not until the development of steel wire in the sixteenth century that knitting could be done by everyone. Although the complexity of the early work shows that skills were of a high order and may have been evolving for some time, the remaining fragments do not give earlier dates. For crochet, the origins may be as late as the nineteenth century, but again this is unclear.

The sheep and shepherd's year

The sheep's year has changed little over millennia. Although some sheep can lamb naturally at any time of year, most ewes lamb in the spring. To do this, they need a ram 150–155 days before they lamb.

SPRING
Usually lambs are born from January to April. Some flocks lamb in the field and stay there, some shepherds bring in the ewes to lamb away from predators in the barn, and some bring in lambs born in the fields for a day or two in the lambing pen to ensure all is well.

Spring on the farm
Shepherds ensure the lambs are healthy and fed, but otherwise leave them to the care of their mothers.

Skilled shearers are always in demand—the best can shear 250 sheep in a day. It's painless for the animals and essential for their welfare.

sending the lambs and any cull animals to slaughter for meat and skins.

Once the sales are over, it's time for tupping: this involves bringing in carefully selected rams to work with the ewes for next year's lambs. The rams stay with the ewes for around six weeks and are then moved to a separate pasture.

Now the ewes are monitored carefully in case they need extra feed. Some ewes are brought in to stay in barns for the winter, or are provided with additional shelter, but most of the native breeds stay out, with perhaps access to a field shelter.

WINTER

For longwool sheep, there may be winter shearing. For sheep to be shown in the spring, there is shearing to get the fleece into the best condition for winning prizes (topiary has nothing to teach a sheep showman!).

Careful monitoring of the ewes, more vaccinations to give some immunity to the lambs when they are born, and extra feed if necessary are all winter activities. A cold winter will result in fewer diseases, but if it is a warm and wet year there is a risk of worms, liver fluke, and even blowfly strike (see page 14).

In the early evening the lambs race around the fields, playing, and then snuggle up to their mothers to sleep. Lambs start to eat a little grass and can be given extra rations to help them grow. The ewes may also need extra feed as they are making milk for their lambs.

SUMMER

This should be an easy time, with grass and lambs growing well, but a watchful eye is needed to repair fences, monitor progress, check and treat against worms, and vaccinate against diseases.

It is also show time! Agricultural shows across the farming world enable shepherds to exhibit their best animals, win prizes, compare notes and enjoy the sun (or suffer the rain, as the case may be).

For most flocks this is a time for shearing. In the south of England, this starts as early as May. As it gets warmer, the shearers move north and by August and September, the sheep in Scotland are being shorn. Many shearers travel the world—it can be summer all year round between the UK, U.S., Australia, and New Zealand if you plan carefully!

AUTUMN

Now is the time for sheep sales: buying and selling ewes, rams, and lambs to invest in the future and also

From shorn fleeces to yarns

For the farmer, the end of the wool story is shearing, rolling, and packing the fleeces into wool sheets—large sacks which take up to 130 lbs (60 kg)—then taking them to the local Wool Board depot, co-operative center or wool mill. For the many smallholders, spinsters, and craft workers who specialize in rare, minority, or local breed wools, this may be the first stage of the job, although some people buy their fleeces at this point.

But it is only the beginning for turning fleeces into yarns and other products. Once at a depot or wool mill, the wool is graded and sometimes sorted to remove anything the farmer should already have removed (vegetation, dags, or poor, dirty or stained fleeces, all of which is better left on the farm for mulch and fertilizer).

Once graded, the wool is scoured (washed) to remove dirt and lanolin. Depending on how much it has rained, which breed produced the wool, and where it was produced, the clean fleece will weigh only half to three-quarters of the original greasy fleece.

After scouring and drying, the wool is ready for processing. It may simply be teased apart, or blended with other fibers for color or performance reasons. It is then carded to separate the fiber into a manageable and even web. Hand-spinners make the web into rolls to draw out for spinning, while machines create a number of individual slubbings, each one rubbed together sufficiently to be able to woolen-spin them on a large spinning frame.

If the yarn is to be worsted-spun, the wool is taken half-carded to a series of machines which align the fibers and comb out all short fiber and any remaining vegetation. This can also be done by hand, using heavy wool combs (such as those used to martyr St. Blaise, the patron saint of wool combers and of a local church near my home in Cornwall).

As the wool is combed, removing air, worsted-spun yarns are less insulating than woolen-spun yarns.

The spun single yarns may then be plied to make a balanced knitting yarn, or remain single to wind on to cones for weavers, or to be cone-wound and steamed for sock or machine-knitting.

Once complete, the yarns may also be dyed. Some yarns are made from fleece which is dyed after scouring, although dyeing finished hanks generally seems to achieve a softer result as far as hand-knitting yarns are concerned.

The original price of the wool, which by now is only about half the weight of the original greasy fiber, will have doubled in terms of raw material content of a finished yarn. It is then multiplied by ten to twenty times (depending on the scale of machine

The wool from Jacob sheep comes in a range of colors which can be spun into single-shade yarns, blended together, or even dyed.

Carding machines use a series of metal teeth to separate the tufts of clean, scoured wool into individual fibers ready for spinning into yarn.

The spun and plied yarn is wound into balls or skeins ready for sale. Dyeing can take place in the fleece or after spinning.

production) for machine-made yarns, and a hundred times, although very rarely achieved by the craft worker, if hand-spun.

It takes an experienced hand-spinner a good hour to make 100 yards (92 meters) of yarn, after doing all the preparation by hand, so she will need three hours for a 3-ply yarn, plus an hour to ply it, to make around one 1.1 oz (50 g) ball of wool. Hand-spun wool is too cheap. And machine-spun wool from small, rare flocks, made in small amounts, is pretty cheap too.

Beyond yarns

Although it has been through all the stages from sheep to a yarn, the wool is still a raw material and has to be made into something—whether knitted, crocheted or woven—and so the yarn is the beginning of the third stage of the life of a fleece, after the farm and the mill.

Apart from single or plied yarns, whether woolen- or worsted-spun, there are many other types: specialist bouclé or single-twist yarns; dyed, marled; tweeded; yarns with glitter, wire, or different types of fiber added, and many more.

As noted above, the yarns may be supplied in several different formats. Usually, a knitting yarn is spun sufficiently only to hold the fibers together, to achieve the softest result (unless going for a specific style, such as a Guernsey yarn). Weaving yarns are made with a much higher twist for added strength so that they do not break under tension in a weaving loom.

Weaving opens a whole other world of technicalities and techniques, particularly the dyeing and finishing of a woven cloth, itself a work of considerable complexity. Could this be your next project?

Carded wool can be made into thin or fat wadding, called batts. It can be used just as wadding or made into felt using individual barbed needles or a needle-felting machine— or by using water, soap, and muscle or machine power. Is this another project for you?

Wool can also be recycled by tearing up spun yarns or woven cloth in a garneting machine. It may be spun on specialist machines capable of spinning very short fibers, or used as wadding or carpet underlay. So wool is not a one-use product either! After its life in the third stage, there is a fourth stage of reuse, recycling, or composting to make nutrition for future generations of sheep.

Fiber facts

This is a very brief glossary of the terms used throughout this book. Together with the individual sections on each sheep breed, its special pattern and the section on Practicals, this should enable you to find and enjoy pure-breed wools, and use them successfully for your projects. If you need more information or clarification, you should be able to find out more about the terms used on the internet or by using some of the books in the bibliography.

In the Practicals section (see page 132), there is more information on knitting yarns and the differences in terminology between different countries when describing yarns. The information below is a very simplified guide and relatively personal, so you may find that others will describe things differently. This is one of the joys and challenges of sheep, wool, yarn, and knitting.

Sheep terminology

AMERICAN LIVESTOCK BREEDS CONSERVANCY: a non-profit membership organization in the U.S. which works to protect more than 180 livestock breeds including sheep. It was founded in 1977.

BLOWFLY STRIKE: attack on a sheep by blue or green blowflies that lay eggs under the skin; after hatching, the larvae eat the flesh of the sheep. If not treated in time, this will kill the sheep.

CROSS-BRED: a sheep with parents of different breeds.

CRUTCHING: trimming off the fleece around the anus and tail to reduce the chance of infection and blowfly strike.

EWE: a female sheep.

EAR-TAGS: a plastic tag, now compulsory in Europe, containing a micro-chip to identify individual sheep. They cause problems in commercial flocks due to additional cost and time required to use them, but they are an essential tool in managing pedigree flocks. Sheep often lose tags, sometimes tearing their ears quite badly, by trying to eat stuff on the other side of fences and then catching the tag on the way back. It is difficult to replace tags in torn ears, though sheep do not seem to care much! Older marking systems, such as that used in Cumbria, consisted of placing notches in the ears to identify the flock owner and age of sheep. Some lambs are spraypainted with supposedly temporary graffiti numbers, which spoils the fleece as it does not wash out.

FLEECE: the growing or shorn wool of a sheep.

FOOTROT: infection in the foot of a sheep causing lameness; often starts with "strip" or soreness due to damp grass, but also caused by numerous bacteria in the soil. It has a distinctive and very unpleasant odor. Can be prevented by using trace minerals and garlic, alongside good and careful hoof trimming, and can be minimized by good observation and prompt treatment.

HOG, HOGGET: a yearling ewe, north of England.

IN-BRED: a cross-bred sheep bred back into the parent ram.

LAMB: a sheep under one year old.

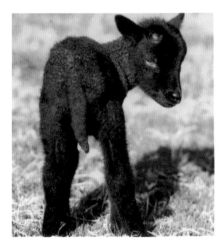

LAMBING: ewes having their lambs.

LIVER-FLUKE: worms that attack a sheep's liver, as part of a cycle from small snails, living in water courses, though the larval stage in the sheep. Sheep can survive this but it does not do their general health status much good and is best avoided or treated promptly.

MOORIT: brown coloring (there are many other Norsk color terms; see Shetland sheep on page 115 for more information).

MULE: a ewe with a mountain or hill sheep mother and a pure-bred father, such as Blue-faced Leicester.

PEDIGREE: a breed society registered pure-bred sheep with (usually) at least three generations of pure-bred parents.

PESTICIDE: insecticide treatments to reduce the likelihood of blowfly strike or to treat it—fleeces treated with such pesticides should not be sent for processing unless there are at least three months between applying the chemical and the date of shearing. These normally contain dye to show they have been used and are not easy to wash out. It is also a growing concern that flies are becoming resistant to worms, but some alternative treatments, such as removing skin around the anus and tail to create hairless scar tissue (mulseing), are not considered welfare-friendly. This is an area of considerable debate.

PINKEYE: contagious eye infection, passed on particularly if feeding area is crowded. If not treated this can result in blindness, but it is easily treated with ointment—first signs are sore or slightly opaque eyes.

POLLED: without horns, e.g. the Cotswold is a polled sheep. Some distinct sheep breeds, such as the Dorset Horn or the Poll Dorset, come in horned and hornless versions.

ORGANIC: specialist, audited husbandry system designed to minimise environmental impacts of farming, for any farm product and processing at every stage.

RADDLE: colored chalk worn in a harness by rams to mark which ewes have been served; will wash out of fleece.

RAM: a male sheep.

RARE BREEDS SURVIVAL TRUST (RBST): a registered charity set up in the UK in 1974 to protect and ensure the future of rare pigs, cattle, horses, and sheep. The charity publishes an annual Watch List, classifying animals according to whether the population is viable or not without support. The RBST has been very successful in encouraging the rehabilitation and development of rare breeds, to the extent that many that were originally classified as endangered or at risk are now off the danger list.

SHEARING: trimming off the whole of a sheep fleece, usually done once a year in summer by professional, highly trained shearers. Shearing competitions do not judge only on speed; any injuries or poor treatment of animals cause a loss of marks in the final scoring. The world record for blade-shearing by hand is around two minutes per sheep, and with a shearing machine is under one minute.

SHEARLING: a yearling ewe, usually south of England.

SHEEP: generic name for woolly animals, originally wild, whose fossilized remains indicate that they have grazed in the British Isles for over 6,000 years. The first sheep appear to have been domesticated in Europe around 6,000 BC.

SHEEPSKIN: the skin of a slaughtered sheep—may be tanned and used for footwear, clothing, and furnishing, and may also be treated to remove the wool, which can then be used for felt or, if long enough, for spinning. Sheepskin without any wool will also make a soft leather.

TUP: a male sheep, usually north of England.

TUPPING: putting the ram with the ewes.

WETHER: a castrated male sheep, used to keep rams company or to manage a few sheep for wool without lambing. Wethers live long and peaceful lives with few concerns except eating and growing wool. There are whole wether flocks specifically kept to grow wool (and possibly mutton) in some countries.

WOOL-SHEET or **WOOL-SACK:** a large bag into which shorn fleeces are packed for storage or transport.

WORMS: a problem to which lambs in particular are susceptible, although adult sheep can carry some and not suffer. Worm treatments have been over-used, resulting in worm populations being increasingly resistant to some types. More careful management is now undertaken.

YOW: a female sheep or ewe, usually north of England.

Wool terminology

Note: unless otherwise stated, micron counts are as defined by British Wool Marketing Board.

AMERICAN SHEEP INDUSTRY ASSOCIATION: represents 82,000 producers in the U.S. Started in 1865.

BRADFORD COUNT: old way to define thickness of fibers. Higher numbers mean finer fibers.

BREED SOCIETY: organisation set up to promote the interests of a sheep breed.

BRITISH WOOL MARKETING BOARD: set up in 1950 to collect, grade, and market all wool from flocks of four sheep or more (except in Shetland).

CAMPAIGN FOR WOOL: set up in 2009 with support of British Wool Marketing Board, Australian Wool Initiative, New Zealand, Norway, and Shetland wool associations and many organizations and businesses. It promotes wool worldwide and organizes annual Wool Week.

COARSE WOOL: 35+ microns (my definition), better for carpets and felt than knitting.

CRIMP: nature of the curls, waves, and crimps in a fleece.

DOWN WOOL: shorter, more bouncy, resilient, and crimped, often non-luster, 31–35 microns.

FELT: fleece or fabric where fibers are matted together.

FINE WOOL: 29–35 microns, usually down or lambs wool, but also native or minority breeds.

HANDLE: magical combination of softness, fineness, luster, length, and health of a fleece. Not easy to define—you know it when you feel it!

HILL WOOL: between mountain and down, around 33 microns.

LAMBS WOOL: wool shorn from sheep under a year old.

LUSTER WOOL: wool with a natural sheen, around 26–35+ microns, often mountain wool.

LONGWOOL: wool which grows to over 10 cm (4 in) in staple length (my definition).

MEDIUM WOOL: 31–35 microns. I would add usually 2–4 in (5–10 cm) long.

MICRON: a thousandth of a millimeter, used to measure the thickness of individual fibers. Human hairs are 40–50 microns; sheep hairs start at 11 microns.

MOUNTAIN WOOL: longer, coarser, with more wave than crimp; 35+ microns.

NEW WOOL: shorn from sheep.

NON-LUSTER WOOL: wool without a natural sheen.

SEMI-LUSTER WOOL: wool with a slight natural sheen.

SHEARLING WOOL: wool shorn from sheep the summer after the year they were born.

SHORT WOOL: averaging less than 2 in (5 cm) in staple length (my definition).

SLIPE WOOL: from slaughtered sheep, mostly used for carpets. Unless label says "pure new wool," some recycled or slipe wool may have been used.

STAPLE: wool fibers as a cluster; includes the length and the way the fibers hold together.

STAPLE LENGTH: the length of the wool from a sheep when straightened without stretching.

WOOL: the hairs that grow on sheep.

Yarn terminology

There are NO yarn standards—partly because wool is a natural fiber—and so this guide is approximate. There is no substitute for following pattern recommendations, tension swatches, and doing a few experiments. Once you are confident, start to knit and see where it takes you.

2-PLY YARN: a fine yarn making 32–34 sts and 40–42 rows for a 4 in (10 cm) square on size 3 (3.25 mm) needles. May be called sock or lace-weight!

3-PLY YARN: around 32 sts and 40 rows for a 4 in (10 cm) square on size 3 (3.25 mm) needles—similar to modern 2-ply yarns.

4-PLY YARN (UK YARN TYPE): originally made by plying four standard yarns together, as with

2-ply and 3-ply, now may also be a 2-ply yarn, two-thirds the thickness of Double Knitting. Equivalent to U.S. Sportweight yarn. Around 28 sts and 36 rows to 4 in (10 cm) square on size 3 (3.25 mm) needles.

ARAN YARN (UK YARN TYPE): thicker than Double Knitting yarn, possibly 25–30% thicker, can be achieved by using two strands of 4-ply yarn, equivalent to U.S. Medium or Fishermans yarn and Australian 12-ply yarn. 17–18 sts to 4 in (10 cm) on size 8–9 (5-5.5 mm) needles.

BULKY YARN: U.S. name for UK Chunky yarn. Slightly thicker—14 sts and 19 rows to 4 in (10 cm) on size 10 (6 mm) needles.

CHUNKY YARN (UK YARN TYPE): thicker than Aran yarn, around twice as thick as Double Knitting. Can be achieved by using two strands of Double Knitting yarn, 15 sts and 20 rows to 4 in (10 cm) on size 10 (6 mm) needles.

COUNT: the thickness of a yarn. May be measured in various ways, usually the thickness (metric count) or weight of a given length of yarn.

DEWSBURY COUNT: traditional standard thickness count for woolen-spun carpet yarns.

DOUBLE KNITTING YARN (UK YARN TYPE): originally a double version of 4-ply yarn but now commonly a 3-ply yarn, equivalent to U.S. Worsted and an Australian 8-ply yarn, 22 sts and 30 rows to 4 in (10 cm) on size 6 (4 mm) needles.

FINGERING (U.S. YARN TYPE): finer yarn, equivalent to UK 4-ply.

GAUGE: see tension.

GUERNSEY (UK YARN TYPE): a specialist fine worsted-spun yarn, in 5 plies, thinner than Double Knitting or Worsted, used for dense, highly textured Guernsey-style pullovers.

LACE-WEIGHT YARN: fine yarn used for lace knitting.

LOPI YARN: an Icelandic wool; not always suitable for wear next to the skin.

METRIC COUNT (NM): modern standard yarn thickness count.

PLY: the twisting of two or more yarns together.

SPECIFICATION: the definition of the particular thickness and ply of a yarn; can also include the number of twists in the ply or single yarn. There are no international or even national standards, so not all 4-ply yarns will be a certain thickness. It is important to remember this and ALWAYS KNIT A TENSION SWATCH if you need things to be exact.

SPORT (US YARN TYPE): finer than Double Knitting, 23–26 sts and 32–34 rows to 4 in (10 cm) on size 3–5 (3.25–3.75 mm) needles.

SUPER-CHUNKY YARN: a very thick yarn, usually specific to the manufacturer, probably around four strands of Double Knitting yarn.

TENSION: the number of stitches (sts) and rows made with a given yarn and given needle size to make a 4 in (10 cm) square. If you have too many stitches and rows, reduce your needle size and try again, or if too few, increase the size.

WOOLEN-SPUN YARN: spun from carded slubbings, the fibers mingle in all directions.

WORSTED (U.S. YARN TYPE): 20 sts and 26 rows to 4 in (10 cm) on size 7 (4.5 mm) needles, equivalent to UK Double Knitting and Australian 8-ply.

WORSTED COUNT: the traditional standard thickness count for worsted spun yarns.

WORSTED-SPUN YARN: spun from combed tops, fibers aligned and short fibers removed.

YARN: a thread made of twisted fibers. (In this book almost all fibers are wool!)

WPI (WRAPS PER IN): a useful way of determining thickness of a yarn and of comparing yarns by wrapping it around a ruler, not too tightly or crammed together (beware of very fluffy yarns when doing this!). On average: Lopi and Bulky yarns will have 5–6 WPI, Chunky 7 WPI, Aran 8 WPI, Knitting Worsted 9 WPI, Double Knitting 11 WPI, Sport weight 12 WPI, 4-ply Fingering 14 WPI, and 3-ply or Baby yarn 16–18 WPI. Remember pure-breed yarns may knit up in different ways because they are designed to give a different effect, and thickness alone is not entirely a good measure. Worsted-spun yarns tend to be leaner than woolen-spun, luster and longwool yarns are also leaner, while downland, fine, and short wools make bulkier yarns.

YORKSHIRE SKEIN WEIGHT (YSW): the traditional thickness count for woolen-spun knitting and weaving yarns.

pure wools
& patterns

Black Welsh Mountain fleece

The Welsh Mountain sheep has been prized for its meat since medieval times. The black strain has existed since the nineteenth century. It can live happily on the high hills of Wales without shelter or supplementary food, surviving in a landscape where no plough or cattle can go.

Welsh Mountain sheep are generally white, and are descended from a breed that dates back to the thirteenth century.

In the nineteenth century, fleeces from Black Welsh Mountain lambs (known as *coch ddu* or reddish brown, the color they turn when they are bleached by the sun) became sought after. As a result, flock masters began to breed black sheep and created a separate, pure strain. The sheep remain black all their lives, unlike Hebrideans which turn gray with age.

However, as reliable black dyes were developed, the fleeces became less valued, and Black Welsh Mountain sheep less common. Recent concerns about the use of chemicals, interest in biodiversity, and the growing popularity of pure wools have helped this breed to become popular again.

Although these small sheep, averaging 99 lbs (45 kg) for an adult ewe, and 132–143 lbs (60–65 kg) for an adult ram, remain common in Wales and are popular with smallholders, the Black Welsh Mountain is not numerous. The Rare Breeds Survival Trust lists fewer than 3,000 registered ewes in the UK. There are approximately 800 animals in over 50 flocks in the U.S. and Canada, where it is listed as a conservation breed. The North American flocks are the descendents of a flock of three rams and 13 ewes imported from Britain in 1973.

BREED AT A GLANCE

Sheep type: Native.
Appearance: Black fleece, long tails, no wool on their neat little faces and legs, as is typical of mountain breeds. The rams have horns, though the ewes normally do not.
Rare breeds status: Classified by the UK Rare Breeds Survival Trust as a Native Breed. American Livestock Breeds Conservancy classes it as Recovering.
Further information:
UK breed society: (www.blackwelshmountain.org.uk).
U.S. breed society: (www.blackwelsh.org).
History: Initially prized for their meat, this separate and pure strain of black sheep was bred in the nineteenth century to satisfy demand for black lamb fleeces.

Aran yarn

raw fleece

4-ply yarn

FLEECE FACT FILE
Fleece weight: 3–4 lbs (1.25–2 kg)
Staple length: 3–4 in (6–10 cm)
Micron count: 32–35 on average
Crimp: Indistinct
Handle: Dense and soft but lofty
Natural colors: Black; fibers may have brown tips where they have been bleached by the sun
Mixed colors: None
Luster: Semi-luster

Close-up of knitted 4-ply sample

carded fleece

DK yarn

scoured fleece

Black Welsh Mountain yarn

Black Welsh Mountain is a versatile, durable wool. Fleeces from lambs and shearlings will happily work as fine as a 4-ply yarn and right up to chunky weight. The wool is not generally suitable for wear next to the skin unless you are less sensitive than the average person (like me!). If you want to do this, look for yarn from younger fleeces where possible.

Black Welsh sheep have been bred to give a fine, soft, and consistent wool. They rarely have coarse, kempy fibers. Lambs' fleeces are usually completely black, though older ones tend to bleach, resulting in off-black or bitter chocolate yarn shades.

Many white Welsh sheep (such as Welsh Mountain, the white Badger Face, and the Llanwenog, a Welsh valley sheep) tend to have black, coarse kemp hairs. It is this particular attribute that gives character to their fleeces, and it becomes more apparent with age. White kemp is more pronounced in the black Balwen, making for a heathery gray-black more suitable for weaving into rugs. If you find a Black Welsh Mountain fleece with more than a small amount of kemp it is probably not completely pure bred.

The yarn—which is soft and warm with a good loft—will cheerfully work in all types of pullovers, waistcoats, jackets, scarves, hats, and mittens. It is also suitable for pillows, shawls and throws, and afghans. Being so soft, it might not

wear as well as Balwen or Badger Face in socks, unless blended with, say, 50 percent mohair.

The following pattern is for a unisex body-warmer or waistcoat, with a ribbed back to help it fit well and keep you warm. However, you could substitute Black Welsh Mountain yarn for the patterns included for Hebridean, Galway, Jacob, Manx Loagthan, Ryeland, and Zwartbles yarns.

Versatile and cozy, the wool from young Black Welsh Mountain sheep (below) can be worn next to the skin while older fleeces bring stitch definition to outerwear (right).

YARN USER'S GUIDE
Good for ...
• Warmth, loft and bulk
• Blending and weaving
• Felt

Not so good for ...
• Inner garments
• Baby clothes
• Dyeing

Cozy body-warmer

By Rita Taylor

This is a neat and simple body-warmer for children, men and women. It has an attractive moss stitch front and a cozy, stretchy rib back to make it fit well, so it needs no waist shaping. The garment may be left open as a loose waistcoat, finished as a true body-warmer with a zip right up to the neck, or you could use horn buttons or toggles and loops for a more casual/retro look.

For an even warmer garment, make two and sew them together to make a double thickness of fabric. Make them in two different colors for a reversible body-warmer, or use a contrasting colored zip and matching blanket stitch for the seams.

Method

BACK (make one)

Using size 6 (4 mm) needles, cast on 70 (80, 90, 100, 110, 120) sts and work in k2 p2 rib until work measures 12 (13½, 14, 14¾, 15¼, 16) in, 30.5 (34.25, 35.5, 37.5, 38.75, 41.75) cm. (Lengthen or shorten as desired.)

Armhole shaping

Bind off 5 sts at beginning of next 2 rows. Decrease 1 st at each end of every alternate row for 4 rows until 56 (66, 76, 86, 96, 106) sts remain.
Work straight until armhole measures 7 (7½, 8, 8¼, 8¾, 9) in, 17.5 (19, 20, 21, 22, 23) cm from decrease.

Shape shoulder

Bind off 9 (11, 13, 14, 16, 17) sts at beginning of next 2 rows and 9 (11, 12, 14, 16, 18) sts at beginning of next 2 rows. Leave remaining 20 (22, 26, 32, 32, 26) sts on holder (for back of neck).

RIGHT FRONT
(make one)

Using 4 mm (size 6) needles, cast on 36 (42, 44, 52, 56, 60) sts. Work in double moss stitch until work measures same as back to armholes.

Armhole

Decrease for armhole at left side only, as for back. Continue until armhole measures 3 (3½, 4, 4¼, 4¾, 5) in, 7.5 (9, 10, 11, 12, 12.75) cm from decrease.

Shape neck

Right side of work facing, bind off next 6 (6, 8, 10, 10, 12) sts. Decrease 1 st at neck edge of every row until 18 (22, 25, 27, 32, 35) sts remain. Continue until armhole measures same as back to shoulder. Bind off 9 (11, 13, 14, 16, 17) sts at

MEASUREMENTS
Around the bust: 26–28 (28–30, 32–34, 36–38, 40–42, 44–46) in (66–71 (71–76, 81–86, 91.5–96.5, 102–107, 112–117) cm)
Garment measurement: 28–30 (30–32, 34–36, 38–40, 42–44, 46–48) in (71–76 (76–81, 86–91, 96.5–101.5, 107–112, 117–122) cm)
Length: 19 (21, 22, 23, 24, 25) in (48 (51, 53.5, 56, 58.5, 61, 63) cm)
Instructions are given for the smallest size first, followed by larger sizes in brackets

NEEDLES & NOTIONS
One pair each size 4 (3.5 mm) and size 6 (4 mm) knitting needles
Stitch holder
Zip or toggles/buttons (optional)

GAUGE
Approx 20 sts x 28 rows = 4 in (10 cm) over stocking stitch on size 6 (4 mm) needles
Adjust needle size to give required tension.

ABBREVIATIONS (see also page 140)
Double moss stitch: Rows 1 and 2: (k2 p2) to end; Rows 3 and 4: (p2, k2) to end.

SKILL LEVEL	

beginning next row and 9 (11, 12, 14, 16, 18) sts at beginning of following alternate row

LEFT FRONT
(make one)

Work as for right front, reversing shapings.

SHOULDER SEAMS

Sew fronts to back along shoulder seams.

NECKBAND

Using size 4 (3.5 mm) needles, pick up and k across 6 (6, 8, 10, 10, 12) sts bind off for neck, pick up and knit 16 (18, 20, 22, 24, 26) sts from right front neck edge, knit 20 (22, 26, 32, 32, 26) sts from stitch holder at back neck, pick up and knit 16 (18, 20, 22, 24, 26) sts from left front neck edge, pick up and knit 6 (6, 8, 10, 10, 12) sts from bind off sts at left neck edge. Work 6 rows in K2 P2 rib. Bind off.

To fit sizes 26–28 (28–30, 32–34, 36–38, 40–42, 44–46) in (66–71 (71–76, 81–86, 91.5–96.5, 102–107, 112–117) cm)

19 (21, 22, 23, 24, 25) in. (48 (51, 53.5, 56, 61, 63.5) cm)

15 (16, 18, 20, 22, 24) in (38 (40.5 45.5, 51, 56, 61) cm)

FINISHING

Sew side seams. Sew in zip or make loops for toggles and sew on toggles. Darn in all loose ends.

Blue-faced Leicester fleece

The Blue-faced Leicester was originally concentrated in the north of England and known as the Hexham Leicester. It is a big, tall sheep, with a very fine long fleece, hanging distinctively in individual neat locks with a tiny crimp. It has no wool on the head and legs, virtually none on the belly, and it does not have the top-knot or fringe typical of the Leicester or Lincoln Longwool.

The fleece of the Blue-faced Leicester is prized for its ability to produce fine, soft, hard-wearing and lustrous yarns. The wool is fine and dense, and spins into a soft yarn.

The sheep has a wide chest, and a long straight back, with the appearance of a square body and legs at the corners. It has the typical Roman nose of the Leicester breed and big hare-like ears.

If left a bit later for shearing, the fleeces peel back from the necks and, to my mind, give these sheep a slightly vulture-like appearance!

The ewes weigh in at around 176 lbs (80 kg) and the rams at 253 lbs (115 kg), making them one of the largest British sheep breeds.

The Blue-faced Leicester is now mainly bred to create "terminal sire" pedigree rams to cross with mountain sheep. The resulting progeny are known as "Mules."

Mule ewes produce strong, fast-growing lambs, while maintaining their dam's hardiness and longevity. Today Mules number half of all crossbred ewes in the UK.

The Blue-faced Leicester is not rare, though it might have a natural tendency to be rare, as it is not known for its hardiness, and some (perhaps prejudiced?) people say all purchases of one of these wonderful sheep should have a spade thrown in for use at burial!

However, this breed has wider appeal. The first Blue-faced Leicester sheep were imported into Canada in 1970 and the first flocks appeared in the U.S. in the 1980s.

BREED AT A GLANCE

Sheep type: Native.
Appearance: Creamy white, with gray skin on the head (hence the name Blue-faced) and an occasional tendency to produce "black" versions. Hornless with a long tail.
Rare breeds status: None.
Further information:
UK breed society: www.blueleicester.co.uk.
U.S. breed societies: www.bflba.com, www.bflsheep.com.
History: The Blue-faced Leicester is a relatively recent sheep. Development was started in eighteeth-century Leicestershire, UK, by Robert Bakewell, as part of his program to breed longwooled sheep, and continued in Northumberland into the early twentieth century.

4-ply yarn

raw fleece

FLEECE FACT FILE
Fleece weight: 2.2–4.4 lbs (1–2 kg)
Staple length: 3–6 in (8–15cm)
Micron count: 26–26.5
Crimp: Fine
Handle: Silky
Natural colors: White, some black and gray
Mixed colors: None
Luster: Semi-luster

scoured
fleece

Close-up of knitted 4-ply sample

carded fleece

DK yarn

Blue-faced Leicester yarn

The drapey, heavy wool of the Blue-faced Leicester sheep makes one of the most popular knitting yarns for those who love soft wool. It is a buttery golden cream in color and has an almost soapy soft texture.

The wool of the Blue-faced Leicester is amongst the finest produced in the UK and is very consistent across the whole body, with no kemp. Due to the fine crimp, the locks appear to be quite short, but stretch out to a staple length of 3–6 in (8–15 cm). It is a very dense fiber, so a small sack will weigh a lot more than one of a similar size containing, say, fleece from Ryeland or Shetland sheep.

Despite its renowned softness, as a semi-luster wool, the yarn made from Blue-faced Leicester sheep is also reasonably hard-wearing. When worsted-spun it also has a lovely sheen and, of course, it dyes well too. As a result the wool is excellent to add to weaving yarns in blends to achieve some luster, dye-friendliness, and drape, and can, for example, be used to maintain the characteristics of mohair yarn, while making adult mohair fiber softer and easier to spin.

Despite their size, Blue-faced Leicesters produce fleeces half the weight of other Leicester breeds. This, and the bare belly, may explain their lack of hardiness. If you are lucky enough to find some "black" fiber, it will not be black at all, but a rich chocolate brown as the fleece bleaches quite heavily in the sun. In fact, a "black" Blue-faced Leicester sheep will only look black around the edges.

The luster of Blue-faced Leicester yarns makes them perfect for textured knitting, as it will emphasize the stitches. Here, we have also taken advantage of its softness to create a baby blanket with a geometric design, and a lacy ladies' sleeveless top. If you want to try other options, substitute Blue-faced Leicester yarn for the patterns shown for Castlemilk Moorit, Corriedale, Gotland, or Manx Loagthan yarns.

Soft and lustrous yarn spun from the fleece of Blue-faced Leicester sheep is ideal for textured stitches and lace knitting where it shows the stitches and openwork patterns to great effect. The knitted garments also drape well.

Scallop shell top

By Rita Taylor

The lacy scallop shell pattern of this sleeveless top is deceptively simple to knit, and the square neckline and garter stitch edges mean there are no tricky decrease rows. Generous side slits make it comfortable to wear.

It knits up well in Blue-faced Leicester or an alpaca or alpaca/shetland yarn.

Method

Tip: To make a neat edge, cast on 2 extra stitches and ALWAYS slip the first stitch and knit or purl the last stitch of every row (but remember to include these stitches when counting for decreases).

SCALLOP SHELL PATTERN

Pattern worked over 15 sts and 12 rows:

Row 1: (k5, k2tog, yf, k1, yf, ssk, k5)

Row 2 and every even row: (p15)

Row 3: (k4, k2tog, k1, yf, k1, yf, k1, ssk, k4)

Row 5: (k3, k2tog, k2, yf, k1, yf, k2, ssk, k3)

Row 7: (k2, k2tog, k3, yf, k1, yf, k3, ssk, k2)

Row 9: (k1, k2tog, k4, yf, k1, yf, k4, ssk, k1)

Row 11: (k2tog, k5, yf, k1, yf, k5, ssk)

Row 12: as row 2

YARN REQUIREMENTS

Blue-faced Leicester worsted-weight/DK yarn

• Total amount of wool by weight and approximate length:

Small: 400 g/952 yds (880 m)

Medium: 450 g/1,071 yds (990 m)

Large: 500 g/1,190 yds (1,100 m)

• You will need around 150 g/357 yds (330 m) extra for the longer version.

BACK (make 1)

Cast on 89 (106, 123) sts on size 5 (3.75 mm) needles. Work in garter stitch for 6 rows increasing 1 st at each end of last row to 91 (108, 125) sts.

Change to size 6 (4 mm) needles and work scallop shells pattern with garter stitch edges and 2 knit sts between each scallop. Therefore:

Row 1: K4, *pattern row 1, k2*

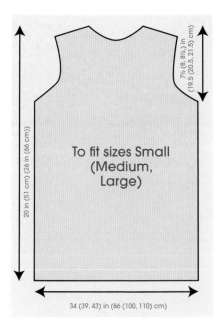

To fit sizes Small (Medium, Large)

20 in (51 cm) (26 in (66 cm))

34 (39, 43) in (86 (100, 110) cm)

7½ (8, 8½,) in (19.5 (20.5, 21.5) cm)

FINISHED SIZES
Garment size: chest 34 (39, 43) in (86 (100, 110) cm; length (neck to hem) 20 in (51 cm) (26 in (66 cm)) for longer version
Instructions are given for the smallest size first, followed by medium and large in brackets.

NEEDLES & NOTIONS
1 pair needles size 6 (4mm)
1 pair needles size 5 (3.75mm)
3 stitch holders
Safety pin

GAUGE
Approx 23 sts x 29 rows = 4 in (10 cm) over scallop shell pattern on size 6 (4 mm) needles.
Adjust needle size to give required tension

ABBREVIATIONS (see also page 140)
ssk: (slip, slip, knit) slip 2 stitches knitwise from the left to the right needle, then insert the tip of the left needle into the fronts of the slipped stitches and knit them together from this position.

SKILL LEVEL

repeat to last 2 sts, k2.
Row 2: K4 *pattern row 2, k2* repeat to last 2 sts, k2.
Thus, the small size will have five scallop pattern repeats, the medium size will have six and the large size will have seven across the width of the garment, plus the 2 k sts between each scallop and the knit stitches at the edges.
Continue with pattern as set until seven patterns repeats have been worked (ten for the longer version).

Armhole shaping
Bind off 7 sts, k14, pattern to last 21 sts, knit to end.
Bind off 7 sts, pattern to end, keeping 2 k sts on either side of scallops. (77 (94, 111) sts).
Working first and last pattern repeats in st st (so that you only have 3 (4, 5) scallops, each with 2 k sts between), decrease on alternate rows as follows:
Row 1: K1, ssk, work to last 3 sts, k2tog, k1.
Row 2: work in pattern as set.
Repeat these 2 rows 4 times (67 (84, 101) sts).
Continue as set, keeping edge sts in st st until armholes measure 7 (7½, 8,) in (18 (19, 20) cm).

Shoulder shaping
Bind off 8 (12, 14) sts at beginning of next 2 rows and 9 (12, 14) sts at beginning of following 2 rows. Leave remaining 33 (36, 45) sts on holder for back neck.

FRONT (make 1)
Work as for back until armholes measure 4½ (5, 5½) in (11 (13, 14) cm, ending with a WS row.

Neck shaping:
Pattern 23 (30, 38) sts, place 21 (24, 25) sts on holder, then pattern to end (24 (31, 38) sts).
Row 1: pattern to last 3 sts, p2tog tbl, p1.
Row 2: k1, ssk, patt to end.
Repeat these 2 rows until 16 (23, 28) sts remain
Continue until work is same length as back. Bind off for shoulder as for back.
Re-join yarn to other side of neck and complete to match, reversing shaping.

MAKING UP
Sew front to back along left shoulder seam.

NECKBAND
With right side of work facing and using size 5 (3.75 mm) needles, pick up and work 33 (35, 45) sts from back neck holder, 17 (21, 25) sts from left front neck edge, 21 (24, 25) sts from front neck holder and 17 (21, 25) sts from right front neck edge. Work 6 rows garter stitch and bind off loosely. Join right shoulder seam and neckband.

ARMBANDS (work 2)
With right side of work facing and using size 5 (3.75 mm) needles, pick up and knit 98 (114, 120) sts along armhole edge.
Work 6 rows Garter Stitch and bind off loosely. Join side seams using mattress stitch leaving 3½ in (9 cm) at hem for side slits.

Baby's log cabin blanket

By Tina Barrett

This subtle blanket design replicates in back-and-forth knitting the traditional pattern of a log cabin quilt in Blue-faced Leicester yarn.

The textured surface is created by using moss stitch for the logs, and stocking stitch for the lines dividing them. To get the pattern to work, you have to count a lot of rows (268 to be precise)! However, the end result is worth it!

Method

Place a stitch marker at the start of every wider 26-row panel.

Using size 6 (4 mm) needles, cast on 203 sts.
Row 1: Moss st 180 sts, k4, moss st 19 sts.
Row 2: Moss st 19 sts, p4, moss st 180 sts.
Repeat rows 1 and 2 for 26 rows.
Row 27: K184 sts, moss st 19 sts.
Row 28: Moss st 19 sts, p184 sts.
Row 29: As row 27
Row 30: As row 28
Row 31: Moss st 157 sts, k4, moss st 19 sts, k4, moss st 19 sts.
Row 32: Moss st 19 sts, p4, moss st 19 sts, p4, moss st 157 sts.
Repeat rows 31 and 32 for 26 rows.
Row 57: K161 sts, moss st 19 sts, k4, moss st 19.
Row 58: Moss st 19, p4, moss st 19, p161.
Row 59: As row 57.
Row 60: As row 58.
Row 61: Moss st 19, k4, moss st 111, *k4, moss st 19* 3 times.
Row 62: *Moss st 19, p4* 3 times, moss st 111, p4, moss st 19.
Repeat rows 61 and 62 for 26 rows.

YARN REQUIREMENTS

Pure Blue-Faced Leicester DK yarn
• Total amount of wool by weight and approximate length
650g/1,547 yds (1,430 m)

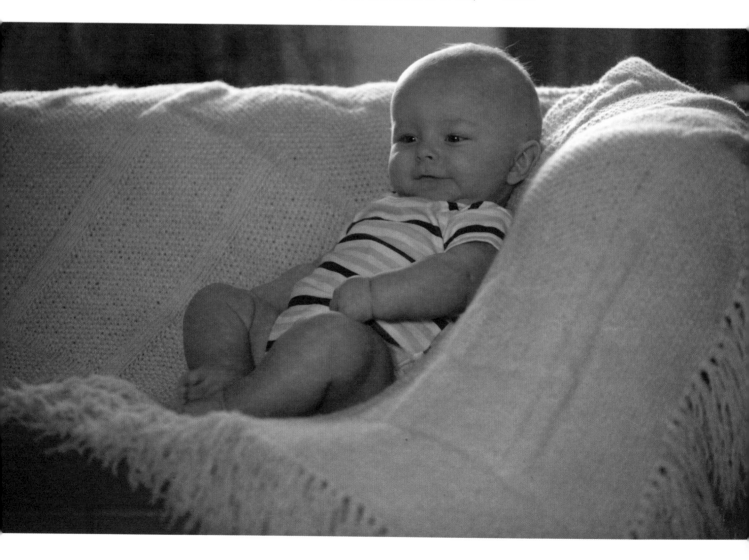

Row 87: Moss st 19, k119, *Moss st 19, k4* twice, moss st 19.
Row 88: Moss st 19, *p4, moss st 19* twice, p119, moss st 19.
Row 89: As row 87.
Row 90: As row 88.
Row 91: *Moss st 19, k4* twice, moss st 65, *k4, moss st 19* 4 times.
Row 92: *Moss st 19, p4* 4 times, moss st 65, *p4, moss st 19* twice.
Repeat rows 91 and 92 for 26 rows.
Row 117: Moss st 19, k4, moss st 19, k73, *Moss st 19, k4* 3 times, moss st 19.
Row 118: Moss st 19, *p4, moss st 19* 3 times, p73, moss st 19, p4, moss st 19.
Row 119: As row 117.
Row 120: As row 118.
Row 121: *Moss st 19, k4* 8 times, moss st 19.
Row 122: Moss st 19, *p4, moss st 19* 8 times.
Repeat rows 121 and 122 for 26 rows.
Row 147: *Moss st 19, k4* 3 times, moss st 19, k50, *Moss st 19, k4* twice, moss st 19.
Row 148: Moss st 19, *p4, moss st 19* twice, p50, moss st 19, *p4, moss st 19* 3 times.
Row 149: As row 147.
Row 150: As row 148.
Row 151: *Moss st 19, k4* 4 times, moss st 42, *k4, moss st 19* 3 times.
Row 152: *Moss st 19, p4* 3 times, moss st 42, *p4, moss st 19* 4 times.
Repeat rows 151 and 152 for 26 rows.
Row 177: *Moss st 19, k4* twice, moss st 19, k96, moss st 19, k4, moss st 19
Row 178: Moss st 19, p4, moss st 19, p96, moss st 19, *p4, moss st 19* twice
Row 179: As row 177.
Row 180: As row 178.
Row 181: *Moss st 19, k4* 3 times, moss st 88, *k4, moss st 19* twice.
Row 182: *Moss st 19, p4* twice,

moss st 88, *p4, moss st 19* 3 times.
Repeat Rows 181 and 182 for 26 rows.
Row 207: Moss st 19, k4, moss st 19, k142, moss st 19.
Row 208: Moss st 19, p142, moss st 19, p4, moss st 19.
Row 209: As row 207.
Row 210: As row 208.
Row 211: *Moss st 19, k4* twice, moss st 134, k4, moss st 19.
Row 212: Moss st 19, p4, moss st 134, (p4, moss st 19) twice.
Repeat rows 211 and 212 for 26 rows.
Row 237: Moss st 19, k184.
Row 238: P184, moss st 19.
Row 239: As row 237.
Row 240: As row 238.
Row 241: Moss st 19, k4, moss st 180.
Row 242: moss st 180, p4, moss st 19.
Repeat rows 241 and 242 for 26 rows.
Bind off in pattern.

FINISHING

Darn in loose yarn ends. Pin and block the blanket to shape. Add fringe to all edges: Cut lengths of yarn 12 in (30 cm) long. Take 3 or 4 strands, fold

MEASUREMENTS
Finished Size: 34 x 44 in (86 x 112 cm) without tassels

SKILL LEVEL

NEEDLES & NOTIONS
One pair size 6 (4 mm) needles
Stitch markers
Crochet hook for tassels

GAUGE
24 sts x 26 rows = 4 in (10 cm) on size 6 (4 mm) needles and working in Log Cabin Pattern stitch.

ABBREVIATIONS (see also page 140)
Moss stitch on even number of stitches (repeat two rows):
Row 1: *k1, p1* repeat from * to * to end of row.
Row 2: *p1, k1* repeat from * to * to end of row.
Moss Stitch on an odd number of stitches (repeat one row):
Row 1: k1, *p1, k1* repeat from * to * to end of row.

in half, then, with RS of work facing, push crochet hook through edge of blanket. Catch hook on looped part of folded bundle and pull everything through the blanket edge. Pull yarn tails over top of right side edge, feed through looped eye of the bundle and pull tight to knot. Space evenly every 4–6 rows/sts.

DESIGNER PROFILE

Tina Barrett has designed knitwear for ten years. She loves working with natural pure wool, particularly for childrenswear. She has created designs for *Cornish Organic Wool*.

Castlemilk Moorit fleece

The Castlemilk was developed to provide decorative grounds management —a task it proved to do well and in a cost-effective manner. As a result of being specially created, it is among the rarest sheep in Britain. It survives thanks to farmers who are dedicated to keeping the breed alive.

The Castlemilk Moorit was "invented" by Sir Jock Buchanan-Jardine to graze parkland on his estate at Castlemilk in Dumfriesshire, Scotland, in the early twentieth century. He wanted brown sheep, so he crossbred brown (moorit) Shetland ewes with Manx Loagthan and wild Mouflon rams. The resulting rams have the show-off spiral horns of a Shetland (the ewes have outward-curved horns), while both rams and ewes have slight white markings from the Mouflon (these are typical of animals bred from relatively primitive origins). Their color, small stature, short tail, and bare legs and heads, come from all three ancestors. As the name suggests, they are mid- or golden brown in color. This is a really small sheep, with adult ewes weighing 77–88 lbs (35–40 kg) and rams only 110–121 lbs (50–55 kg).

When Sir Jock Buchanan-Jardine died in 1970, his flock was culled and dispersed, but one of today's rare breed heroes, Joe Henson, bought six ewes and a ram for his Cotswold Farm Park in Gloucestershire, UK. Thanks to this, and with the support of a few other buyers, the breed has survived.

Today it is popular with smallholders and crafters in the UK and there are also flocks in Belgium and the Netherlands. However, it remains among the rarest of British sheep. It is classified by the Rare Breeds Survival Trust as Vulnerable, with only around 900 registered breeding ewes.

BREED AT A GLANCE

Sheep type: Short-tailed.

Appearance: Short tails and horns in both ewes and rams; the ewes' horns curve outwards while the rams' sport show-off spirals. Mid-brown or golden-brown in color with some slight camouflage white patches.

Rare breeds status: UK Rare Breeds Survival Trust classify it as Vulnerable.

Further information: UK breed society: www.castlemilkmoorit.co.uk.
Belgian breed society: www.castlemilkmoorit.be.

History: Developed by Sir Jock Buchanan-Jardine to graze the parkland on his estate at Castlemilk in Dumfriesshire in the early twentieth century.

raw fleece

scoured fleece

FLEECE FACT FILE
Fleece weight: 2–3 lb (1 kg) or less
Staple length: 2–3 in (5–7.5 cm) or less
Micron count: 30–31.5 (up to 40)
Crimp: High
Handle: Medium
Natural colors: Light to medium brown, tips usually bleached cream by the sun
Mixed colors: None
Luster: Semi-luster

carded fleece

Close-up of knitted DK sample

DK with silk and alpaca yarn

4-ply with silk and alpaca yarn

Castlemilk Moorit yarn

The fleece of the Castlemilk Moorit has a wide range of fiber thickness from fine to coarse, probably due to the way it has been bred with other breeds to increase its numbers. Like many primitive breeds, if left to their own devices they will shed their fleeces rather than wait for shearing.

Although said to be soft, silky and fine, Castlemilk Moorit fleece is also often very short, and usually quite bitty. The crimp is relatively indistinct and fluffy, with the brown fiber bleached to cream at the tips by the sun and weather. With only rarely more than 2.2 lbs (1 kg) from each animal, it is too short to spin as a pure fiber commercially, although this can be done by hand (but it is best attempted by experienced hand-spinners).

There is little kemp, except in older animals on the back legs, and the fleece can be roo'd (combed or plucked out with the fingers) as an alternative to shearing. The yield on spinning short fleeces is much lower than for long fleeces, and Castlemilk Moorit is only suitable for woollen spinning, not worsted.

The sweater design included here uses my commercial yarn. I normally blend the Castlemilk Moorit fibers with 10% tussah silk and 10% alpaca of a similar color: used alone the silk tends to swamp and overcome the fleece characteristics, and the alpaca helps to bring back the natural brown color due to the additional bleaching effect of the pale cream of the silk. We make it in 4-ply and Double Knitting, but it might also work in thicker yarns spun as a pure version (note to self: try this sometime!).

By mixing young fleeces with silk and alpaca the wool can be worn next to the skin. If you would like to try other projects, this yarn is also suitable for anything made from Manx Loagthan, to which it is very similar, and also Black Welsh Mountain, Ryeland, or Zwartbles.

As a Castlemilk Moorit fleece will not yield a lot of yarn, it may make sense to use it with wool from another breed. Here it has been combined with white Jacob yarn dyed red.

YARN USER'S GUIDE
Good for ...
- Weaving (suitable for weft only)
- Clothing
- Felting
- Blending (I find blending with silk and alpaca works well)

Not so good for ...
- Dyeing, although shades that combine with its natural color are successful
- Weaving alone or where strength is needed

Cable and rib sweater

by Sue Blacker and
Myra Mortlock

This pretty ribbed sweater offers a modern twist to classic cable designs, and the pattern includes plenty of options to enable you to personalize the fit and decoration.

The dramatic cable pattern on the front can be given a border of ribbing or moss or seed stitch; the ribs and cables can be twisted— or not—as desired. The ribbed sleeves include three lines of twisted rib.

The basic pattern is a one-size garment, which can be knitted as a cropped or as a longer length. The drop-shoulder, set-in sleeves reach the wrist, or can be lengthened to cover the hand or turned back to create a cosy cuff. If you prefer a shorter, bracelet sleeve, make them a few inches shorter. The high neck can be changed to a shorter turtleneck if you desire.

The sweater shown in the photographs was knitted on one size of needles throughout, and these are the instructions given in the pattern. However, for a firmer, stretchier rib at the hem, cuffs and neck, use needles a size smaller for these, and change to the larger size for the body and sleeves.

Further variations are given on pages 37 and 38.

YARN REQUIREMENTS

Castlemilk Moorit with alpaca and silk worsted-weight/DK yarn
• Total amount of wool by weight and approximate length
Cropped sweater: 500 g/1,119 yds (1,100 m)
Longer sweater: 650 g/1,547 yds (1,430 m)
• Add 50g/119 yds (110 m) for turtle neck if desired

Method

Tip: For a neat side edge, cast on extra 1 st at each end of the row and slip the first stitch and knit the last stitch of every row. (But remember to count them!)

Tip: Check the variations section (pages 38 and 39) as they may affect yarn required and start of back and front.

BACK (make 1)

With size 7 (4.5 mm) needles cast on 112 sts by cable cast on method.
Begin 3x2 rib pattern:
Row 1: K2 (p3, k2) repeat to end.
Row 2: (p2, k3) repeat to last 2 sts, p2.
Repeat until work measures 10 (16) in (26 (40) cm).

Shape underarm
Tip: To minimise the "stepping" effect of shaping, slip through

MEASUREMENTS
Instructions are given for the cropped sweater first, followed by the longer version in brackets.
Garment size: chest 42 in (106 cm) when pressed.
Length from back neck to hem 17 (24) in (43 (60) cm).

NEEDLES & NOTIONS
1 pair size 7 (4.5 mm) needles
Cable needle
2 stitch holders or spare needles
Stitch markers (or waste yarn)

GAUGE
Approx 21 sts x 22 rows = 4 in (10 cm) over 3x2 rib (RS: k2, p3, k2, p3 RS and WS: p2, k3) on size 7 (4.5 mm) needles
Adjust needle size to give required tension

ABBREVIATIONS (see also page 140)
P2togtbl: p2 sts together through the back of the loop (rather than the front).
T4L: (twist 4 sts to the left): slip next 3 sts onto cable needle and hold at front of work, p next st, then k3 from the cable needle.
T4R: (twist 4 sts to the right): place next st on to cable needle and hold at back of work, k3, then p1 from the cable needle.
C6F: slip next 3 sts onto cable needle, hold at front of work. K3, then k stitches from cable needle.
C6B: slip next 3 sts onto cable needle, hold at back of work. K3, then k stitches from cable needle.
TWL: k into the back of the 2nd st on left hand needle, then into the front of the 1st st, taking the 2 sts off together.
TWR: k into the front of the 2nd st on left hand needle, then into the front of the 1st st, taking off the 2 sts together.

SKILL LEVEL

back of the first stitch you are going to bind off.

Bind off 5 sts at start of next 2 rows, 3 sts at start of next 2 rows and 1 st at start of next 10 rows. 86 sts remain.
Continue without further shaping until work measures 17 (23) in (43 (59) cm) from cast on edge.

Shape the shoulders
Work 30 sts. Turn and work back along these 30 sts as follows: slip 1st stitch, k1, psso and work to end of row.
At shoulder edge bind off 9 sts, work to neck edge.
Repeat last 2 rows then dec once more at neck edge.

At shoulder edge bind off remaining sts.
Place center 26 sts on a stitch holder.
Rejoin yarn to the remaining sts and complete the other side of the neck and shoulder, reversing the shaping.

FRONT (make 1)

The front features a central panel worked as follows: a central twisted cable panel of 26 sts on a reverse st st background of 6 sts at each side, making a total of 38 sts. The rib columns on either side of the panel may be twisted. With size 7 (4.5 mm) needles cast on 112 sts.

Row 1: Work in 3x2 rib as for front for 37 sts. Set sts for center panel: p6 for background (reverse stocking stitch), p1, T4L, T4R, p8, T4L, T4R, p1, p6 for background (reverse stocking stitch). Rib as before to end. Maintaining the rib and reverse st st background to the cable panel, work 36 rows of cable panel. Repeat until front measures 10 (16) in (25 (40) cm) from cast on edge.

Instructions for cable panel
Row 2: K2, p6, k10, p6, k2.
Row 3: P2, C6F, p10, C6F, p2.
Row 4: as row 2.
Row 5: P1, T4R, T4L, p8, T4R, T4L, p1.
Row 6: K1, p3, k2, p3, k8, p3, k2, p3, k1.
Row 7: T4R, p2, T4L, p6, T4R, p2, T4L.
Row 8: P3, k4, p3, k6, p3, k4, p3.
Row 9: K3, p4, T4L, p4, T4R, p4, k3.
Row 10: P3, k5, p3, k4, p3, k5, p3.
Row 11: T4L, p4, T4L, p2, T4R, p4, T4R.
Row 12: K1, p3, k5, p3, k2, p3, k5, p3, k1.
Row 13: P1, T4L. p4, T4L, T4R, p4, T4R, p1.
Row 14: K2, p3, k5, p6, k5, p3, k2.
Row 15: P2, T4L, p4, C6B, p4, T4R, p2.
Row 16: K3, p3, k4, p6, k4, p3, k3.
Row 17: P3, (T4L, p2, T4R) twice, p3.
Row 18: K4, p3, (k2, p3) 3 times, k4.
Row 19: P4, T4L, T4R, p2, T4L, T4R, p4 .
Row 20: K5, p6, k4, p6, k5.
Row 21: P5, C6F, p4, C6F, p5.
Row 22: as row 20.
Row 23: P4, T4R, T4L, p2, T4R, T4L, p4.
Row 24: as row 18.
Row 25: P3, (T4R, p2, T4L) twice, p3.
Row 26: as row 16.
Row 27: p2, T4R, p4, C6B, p4, T4L, p2.
Row 28: as row 14.
Row 29: P1, T4R, p4, T4R, T4L, p4, T4L, p1.

Row 30: as row 12.
Row 31: T4R, p4, T4R, p2, T4L, p4, T4L.
Row 32: as row 10.
Row 33: K3, p4, T4R, p4, T4L, p4, k3.
Row 34: as row 8.
Row 35: T4L, p2, T4R, p6, T4L, p2, T4R.
Row 36: as row 6.

Shape underarm as given for **back**. Continue in pattern until front measures 16.6 (22.5) in (40 (56) cm).

Neck shaping
Work 33 sts and turn.
Row 1: sl 1, k1, psso, work to end.
Row 2: work to last 2 sts, k2 tog. Repeat these 2 rows. 29 sts. Now decrease on right side rows only until 27 sts remain.

Shoulder shaping
Bind off 9 sts at armhole edge on next and following alternate row. Do not decrease at neck edge.
On next alternate row bind off remaining sts. Place central 20 sts on a holder.
Rejoin yarn to remaining sts and complete second shoulder, reversing shaping.

SLEEVES (make 2)

These instructions are for sleeves which end at the tip of the thumb without a turned-back cuff. To shorten the cuffs, reduce welt to 3 in (7 cm).

With size 7 (4.5 mm) needles cast on 52 sts.
Work 2x2 rib, twisting all rib lines on right side of work, using TWR for one sleeve and TWL for the other to make them symmetrical, for 5 in (12 cm), ending with right side row.
With wrong side facing, increase 1 st in all the knit stitch ribs to create 3x2 rib.
With right side facing, continue

in 3x2 rib but maintain twisted ribs in 3 center rib lines only. Increase at both ends of next and every following 4th row until you have 102 sts. Periodically mark increase rows with stitch markers or thread for accurate joining.
Continue to knit without shaping until sleeve measures 21 in (53 cm) or desired length, from cast on edge.
Bind off 5 sts at the beginning of the next 4 rows.
Bind off remaining 82 sts.

MAKING UP

Join right shoulder. WS facing, pick up sts around neck *without knitting*: side of back neck 5 sts, stitch holder 26 sts, other side back neck 5 sts, side front neck 18 sts, front stitch holder 20 sts, side front neck 15 sts. (89 sts).
RS facing, at front neck edge, knit and increase as follows: (K1 from needle, k1 from below next st, P2). Repeat 4 times. Work sts from holder in 2x2 rib. Increase in side neck as before to shoulder seam. Back neck (k1, k1 below st, p2) twice. Work 3x2 rib across sts from holder. Finish other side in same way.
Next row, wrong side, work all sts as they present themselves.
Next row: Continue in 2x2 rib, twisting sts if desired.
Work 1 in (2.5 cm) in chosen pattern. Bind off loosely.
Join second shoulder, sew in sleeves, allow underarm body sides to wrap 1 in (2.5 cm) around sleeve top, and all other seams. Block.

VARIATIONS

For a more generous fit: work center panel as given, but the remainder of front, back and sleeves in seed st or moss st with three-line rib panels at the center of the sleeves and a five-line rib at center of back of sweater.

KNITTER PROFILE

Alison Casserly is passionate about knitting and has many years' experience in knitting and crochet. With a BA Honors in Fashion Knitwear & Knitted Textiles, she enjoys experimenting with the natural dye-stuffs she finds near her home.

TO KNIT SLEEVES FROM SHOULDER

With right sides together, sew one shoulder seam, matching rib lines. Open work out. Starting from the 3 st bind-off on body, mark sections as follows: 4 each on back and front with 10 sts to each section. Allow for 2 extra k sts at shoulder seam for center line of sleeve.

Starting with 2 k sts, pick up and work 3x2 rib along 40 sts to shoulder, work 2 center k sts then 40 sts in 3x2 rib to other armhole decrease, turn, cast on 5 sts. Work in pattern to row end. Repeat this row 3 more times. Continue to work down sleeve in 3x2 rib (with three twisted ribs at center) without shaping for 6 rows.

Decrease at both ends of next and every 4th row until 66 sts remain. For precise joining, mark some decreases. Continue until work measures 16 in (40 cm).

To work the cuffs: With wrong side facing, k2tog in all 3st. ribs to give 2 by 2 rib. Right side facing, work twisted rib on knit sts across the whole row. Continue in twisted (2x2) rib for 5 in (12 cm). Bind off.

For a larger size: add 10 sts to front and back i.e. one 3x2 rib repeat on both sides of center panel. Add 2 (2, 1) sts in that sequence to shoulder bind offs and (1¼ in) 3 cm to the length. The cropped version cannot be made any larger than this. The sleeve opening and sleeve should be made following the existing instructions. You will need an extra 50 g/119 yards (110 m) of yarn.

For a smaller size: use size 5 (3.75 mm) needles or reduce number of sts in front and back by 10 each per 8 in (20 cm) reduction (two 3x2 ribs to maintain symmetry).

For a turtle neck: work neck as given for 2 in (5 cm) in 2x2 rib, then change to 3x2 at fold over. Arrange ribs to match front (twist ribs if preferred). Work a further 3 in (8 cm), or more for a deep turtle neck. Allow an extra 50 g/119 yards (110 m) of yarn.

22.5 in (57 cm)

10 (11) in (24 (26) cm)

5 in (12 cm)

17.5 in (45 cm)

20 (27) in (50 (66) cm)

21 in (53 cm)

Cropped (longer) sweater

The cable panel was derived from the Harmony Guide to Aran and Fair Isle Knitting, edited by Debra Mountford. ISBN 0-517-88405-4

For a longer welt to match the cuffs: for back and front, cast on using a size smaller needles and work 3x2 or twisted rib for the first 6 in (14 cm). Change to size 7 (4.5 mm) needles and start cable pattern. Continue pattern above to underarm. If using twisted rib for the sleeve cuffs, either use twisted rib across the welts or use 3x2 rib for the back and sides of the front and twisted rib for the sts which will be below the cable on the front. You will need an extra 100 g/238 yards (220 m) of yarn. It may be best to buy extra as twisted rib can use more yarn.

Corriedale/Falklands fleece

Originally bred in New Zealand, the Corriedale is found all over the world, from Latin America to Australia and Europe, and can live on many types of terrain. Today, the majority are no longer pure-bred, and are likely to have proportions of Merino in them. They are sturdy, medium-sized sheep with bulky, fine fleeces.

Any description of these sheep is something of a history of British colonial sheep development: our "Corriedale" is really generic Falklands wool, which is cross-bred and includes Polwarth, Merino, Coopworth, and Corriedale genes.

As with the Castlemilk Moorit, Blue-faced Leicester, and many more, the Corriedale owes its origin to some men with a mission—in this case James Little, at the North Otago Station, and William Soltau Davidson at Levels Station, on New Zealand's South Island. Between 1868 and 1874 both men concentrated on breeding sheep with consistently high quality fleeces. By the 1890s the Corriedale had become the country's first "native" breed.

They can be large sheep, ranging from 130–180 lbs (60–80 kg) in ewes and from 175 lbs up to even 275 lbs (79–125 kg) in rams. It is still a popular sheep in New Zealand and is also found in North and South America (it was first introduced to the U.S. in 1914), Australia, and Eastern Europe as well as the Falkland Islands.

There are around 2.8 million Corriedales in New Zealand, although this is only 5–6 per cent of the total sheep population. However, you may struggle to find a true Corriedale due to the variations now available.

The fleece is known for its soft, finely crimped staples. It is versatile and makes an excellent hand-knitting yarn, as well as being woven to make medium-weight coats and jackets, worsteds, and light tweeds.

BREED AT A GLANCE

Sheep type: Inbred crossbreed from Merino with Romney or Lincoln.

Appearance: Corriedales are medium-sized white sheep, with a thick fleece, no horns, a top-knot of wool on the head, wool on their legs, and black noses.

Rare breeds status: None.

Further information:
US breed society: www.americancorriedale.com.
Australian breed society: www.corriedale.org.au.

History: Originally developed in New Zealand, the Corriedale was the first of a family of breeds grown for their wool.

4-ply dyed olive yarn

4-ply dyed turquoise yarn

scoured fleece

FLEECE FACT FILE
Fleece weight: 10–13 lbs (4.5–6 kg)
Staple length: 3–5 in (7.5–12.5 cm)
Micron count: 20–30
Crimp: Detailed and wavy
Handle: Dense, medium-fine
Natural colors: Very white (not cream)
Mixed colors: Gray and beige
Luster: Semi-luster

carded long staples

Close-up of knitted DK sample

Pure DK yarn

Corriedale/Falklands yarn

If you want an easy-to-work-with, versatile, soft, semi-lustrous fleece, it is hard to beat Falkland Corriedale wool, which will cater for everything from baby clothes to rugs and afghans. The light bulkiness gives warmth and felts well.

Corriedale/Falklands wool is soft, very white, and bulky, so that it makes yarns which seem fatter than others of the same specification—a 4-ply can knit up almost to resemble a DK yarn.

This wool is good for hand, worsted or woolen spinning, and felting. As it helps mohair hold together, we use ten per cent Corriedale in mohair knitting yarns. The fleece has a detailed, wavy crimp, which is distinct and not fluffy. However, you will find finer, coarser, longer, and shorter Corriedale around the world.

The only drawback is that the fleece is so white that it almost appears (horror of horrors) as if it were synthetic when dyed! This is why we often blend it with a little fine Manx Loagthan, Black Welsh Mountain, or Hebridean fleece to create

a more subtle color. We have yet to find black and gray Corriedales. Because Corriedale is mainly farmed commercially in large flocks, any colored lambs will be selected out very quickly.

For this soft, bulky yarn, we have created a design for a hot-water bottle cover. But you can use it for any of the Black Welsh Mountain, Castlemilk Moorit, Manx Loagthan, North Ronaldsay, Ryeland, or Zwartbles designs in this book.

Pure Corriedale/Falklands yarn lends itself well to blending and dyeing. Its evenness, softness, and bulk makes it suitable for many craft projects. Use it to make knitted garments that are warm but not heavy to wear.

Corriedale hot-water bottle cover

By Sue Blacker

YARN REQUIREMENTS
Corriedale worsted-weight/DK yarn
• Total amount of wool by weight and length for a standard-sized hot-water bottle approximately 3 differently colored 50 g/119 yds (110 m) balls (e.g. 1 purple, 1 pink and 1 gray or 1 turquoise, 1 blue and 1 gray, or 1 white, 1 gray, 1 fawn).

On a cold winter's night there's nothing better than curling up with a hot-water bottle with a cozy knitted cover. This design uses three colors of yarn to create narrow stripes each made up of two differently colored yarns, while a combination of knit and purl stitches makes a stretchy rib pattern.

The cover is made to measure and so you need to measure your bottle and calculate the number of stitches you need to cast on. Instructions for this are given under Method.

By making narrow stripes there is no need to break and rejoin the yarn to create the pattern. Instead, you can just carry the spare color up the side of the work. If you want to adapt the pattern to make wider stripes, you will need to sew or weave in the loose ends afterward to make things neat—use a large-eyed darning needle for this and weave in the ends along the edge of the knitting, so that each end is hidden in a stripe of the same color. If you prefer to make a different pattern, remember that you need to have the same number of rows in each color to use up all three balls evenly.

NEEDLES & NOTIONS
1 pair size 10 (6 mm)
needles

GAUGE
Not necessary as this item
is made to measure.

ABBREVIATIONS
(see page 140)

Method

Measuring the bottle

Measure the hot water bottle,
or copy the dimensions of an
existing cover.

To calculate the width of the
knitting, measure the width of
your bottle and add 2 in (5cm).
For example, if the bottle is 10
in (25 cm) wide, your knitting
will be 12 in (30 cm) wide (10 in
plus 2 in (25 cm plus 5 cm)).

Now calculate the overall
length of the cover. Measure the
length of the bottle, excluding
the neck and spout. You will
knit a piece of fabric this size to
make the first side, then bind off
enough central stitches to leave
a gap for the neck, and cast
them on again in the next row,
to create a slit. The second side
needs to be long enough to go
around the base of the bottle
and come up 4 in (10 cm) on
the other side to enclose the
bottle once you have sewn it
up. It will work like the flap of a
pillowcase, and you can add
buttons and loops to it if you
wish.

Cover (knit 1)

**For tips on color knitting see
page 78.)**
Using size 10 (6 mm) needles
and two colors of yarn (colors A
and B), cast on 7 sts loosely for
every 2 in (5 cm) of your width

measurement (e.g. if the width
is 8 in (20 cm), cast on 28 sts; if 6
in (15 cm), then it cast on 21 sts;
if 10 in (25 cm), 35 sts, etc.).
**N.B. This pattern only works
with multiples of 4 stitches
plus 1**, so if necessary add
an extra stitch to make it work
(e.g. for 6 in (15 cm), you would
need 21 stitches, so there's no
need to add more, but for 28
and 35 stitches, make it 29 and
37, etc.).
Row 1: SL1, *k2, p2*, repeat
from * to * to last 4 sts, k2, p1, k1.
Work all following rows as Row
1, using tweed stripe pattern
and shaping as described
below.
Start in your first two colors (A
and B, whichever of the three
you prefer), work 2 rows, then
drop A and add in the third
color, C. Knit 2 rows, then drop
B and add in A again. Work 2
rows. These six rows set the stripe
pattern: rows 1 and 2, A and B; 3
and 4, B and C; 5 and 6, C and
A and ensure that the ends and
balls of wool are always on the
same side of your work.
Continue stripe and rib pattern
until work is long enough to
cover the length of the hot-
water bottle plus a little easing
(an additional 2 rows).

Create an opening for the
neck of the bottle

Row 1: bind off the middle third

of stitches, continue to end.
Row 2: cast on middle third
stitches, continue to end.
Continue to work, maintaining
the stripe and rib pattern, until
the work will wrap around the
bottle. Knit a further 6 in
(15 cm). Bind off.

To make a collar for the neck
of the bottle

Using size 10 (6 mm) needles
and two colors of yarn pick up
and knit the stitches around the
neck slit.
You can work each side
separately using standard
needles, or work in the round
with double-pointed or circular
needles.
Work the collar in k1, p1 rib,
maintaining the striped pattern.
Continue until the collar is twice
the length of the neck so that
it can be folded back. Bind
off in rib and sew in the ends
securely. Sew up the seams
if each side has been
worked separately.

MAKING UP

Fold the cover so that the
bottom flap is bent backwards
and stitch seams firmly. Turn it
inside so that the flap covers
the base of the hot-water bottle.
The rib pattern is the same on
both sides, so there is no right or
wrong side until it is sewn up.

Cotswold fleece

A big, old sheep! The Cotswold is said to be descended from animals brought to Britain by the Romans. It is certainly a long-standing resident. In medieval times it funded the imposing "wool churches" of the Cotswolds area. Sadly, a great past has not heralded a great present, and it is now a rare breed.

The golden lanolin in the creamy lustrous wool, and the profits made from the fleeces, earned this imposing sheep the title of "Cotswold Lion." A truly beautiful luster longwool, it should ideally be sheared twice a year to improve fleece quality.

The fleece is quite coarse in adults, and benefits from worsted spinning to soften it, but it does not contain any kemp. The staple length depends on whether it is shorn once or twice.

The Cotswold is not as tall as a Blue-faced Leicester but is considerably heavier, at up to 250–275 lbs (113–135 kg) in rams and 200–250 lbs (90–113 kg) in ewes. Their faces are slightly smiling, and their eyes are almost obscured when in full fleece with top-knot and fringe.

The U.S. breed society says it was introduced to the U.S. in 1832, and by 1879 it was the most popular breed in the country with over 760,000 recorded by 1914. It remained popular until the introduction of Merinos from Australia. By the 1980s there were fewer than 600 in the UK and U.S. together.

Today, the Cotswold is designated as At Risk by the Rare Breeds Survival Trust, with less than 1,500 registered breeding ewes. The slow growing nature of this breed means that it is not seen as commercial for meat, while the wool, although long, thick, and strong, has suffered with falling demand for carpets in recent years. Nevertheless, the efforts of rare breed enthusiasts have stablized the flock and it has a better outlook for the future.

BREED AT A GLANCE

Sheep type: Longwool.
Appearance: A big, broad and strongly built sheep without horns.
Rare breeds status: At Risk in the UK; Threatened in the US.
Further information:
UK breed society: www.cotswoldsheepsociety.co.uk.
US breed societies: www.cotswoldbreedersassociation.org, www.CotswoldSheep.us.com and www.cotswoldsheep.us.com/black_cotswolds.
History: Said to be descended from the sheep brought to Britain by the Romans, but may be earlier, and was the basis of the English medieval wool trade.

DK dyed guava
pink yarn

FLEECE FACT FILE
Fleece weight: 9–15 lbs (4–7 kg)
Staple length: 7–12 in
(17.5–30 cm)
Micron count: 34–40
Crimp: Wavy curls
Handle: Heavy and lustrous
Natural colors: Creamy white
Mixed colors: None
Luster: High

natural DK
yarn

DK dyed
moss green
yarn

Close-up of natural DK sample

scoured fleece

raw fleece

carded fleece

Cotswold yarn

The creamy, lustrous wool of the Cotswold sheep is versatile, drapey and hard-wearing. It is also very strong—it can be used for socks and accessories as well as fine garments.

Cotswold wool is very hard-wearing and is ideal for carpets. Long, lustrous Cotswold wool was used to produce broadcloth and army uniforms (it felts well when woven to create a warm and water-resistant greatcoat).

Worsted-spun yarns are lean, shiny, and creamy in their natural state, and bright when dyed thanks to the luster, producing clear, vibrant colors.

Washed, individual locks of the fleece can be used for dolls' hair, Santa Claus beards, or they can be used in their natural state, or dyed, to decorate craft items.

The yarns are slightly fluffy, so a garment will gently felt over time to fill in the gaps

between stitches. However, they are well suited to elegant, lacy, and drapey styles, such as the cable pullover pattern shown here. Other good projects would include those used for Gotland yarns, socks, bags (particularly if made large and then felted), or yarns containing mohair. Or try it with a pattern designed for Blue-faced Leicester—you will get a good, but differently textured, result.

When in full fleece, the top knot and fringe can obscure the eyes of Cotswold sheep (right). The wool dyes well— here moss green and guava pink have been used (below).

YARN USER'S GUIDE
Good for ...
- Outerwear, accessories
- Felting
- Carpets
- Spinning and dyeing
- Garments requiring drape
- Hard-wearing garments

Not so good for ...
- Textured stitches
- Warmth and loft

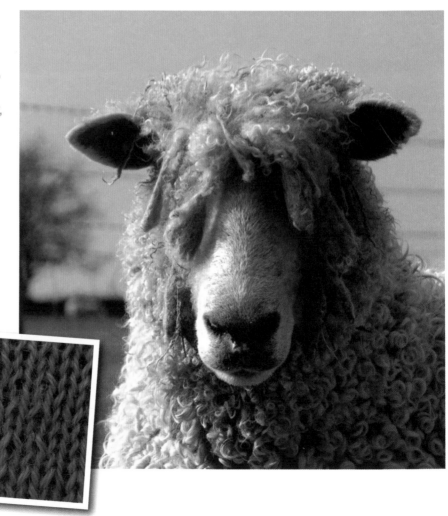

Wavy cable jumper

By Amanda Jones

This attractive and feminine pullover, worked in the round in reverse stocking stitch, has a simple cable with a double wavy-lines design up the front and clever cables worked into the raglan shaping for the arm seams. It has a funnel neck and a small welt but no cuffs, and the ends of the sleeves curl inwards. It has a slightly gauzy texture to optimize the sheen and fineness of the worsted-spun Cotswold yarn.

Method

LOWER BODY
(make one)
Using size 5 (3.75 mm) circular needle cast on 198 (214:230:254) sts, being very careful not to twist the sts join into a ring and work pattern as follows.

Set up round
1st and 4th sizes only: K2 (-:-:1), (p5, k3) five (-:-:7) times, p5, k4, (p1, k4,(p5, k3) five (-:-:7) times, p5, k2 (-:-:1), place SM, k1 (-:-:2), (p5, k3) eleven (-:-:14) times to last sts: p5, k1 (-:-:2) place 2nd SM.

2nd and 3rd sizes only: P 0 (3:1:-), (k3, p5) 0 (6:7:-) times, k4, p1, j4, (p5, k3) 0 (6:7:-) times, p 0 (3:1:-), place SM, p – (2:4:-), (k3, p5) 0 (12:12:-) times to last sts: k3, p – (2:4:-), place 2nd SM.

All sizes
(Front section 103 (111:123:133), back section 95 (103:107:121) sts.)

YARN REQUIREMENTS
Pure Cotswold worsted-spun DK in natural or dyed shades
• Total amount of wool by weight and approximate length:
Small: 450 g/1,070 yds (990 m)
Medium: 500 g/1,190 yds (1,100 m)
Large: 550 g/1,309 yds (1,210 m)
Extra large: 600 g/1,428 yds (1,320 m)

MEASUREMENTS
Around the bust:

30-32 (34-36:38-40:42-44) in
(76-78 (86-92:96-101:106-112) cm)
Garment measurement: 33 (37.5:40.5:45) in (84 (95:103:114) cm)
Length to shoulder: 21.5 (21.5:22:22.5) in (55(55:56:57) cm)
Sleeve seam: 17.5 (17.5:17.75:18) in (44 (44:45:46) cm)

NEEDLES & NOTIONS
1 set size 5 (3.75 mm) circular needle 40 in (100 cm) long
1 set size 3 (3.25 mm) circular needle 30 in (80 cm) long
1 pair size 5 (3.75 mm) needles
Cable needle
4 stitch markers

GAUGE
Approx 21sts and 32 rows = 4 in (10 cm) over st st on size 5 (3.75 mm) needles.
Adjust needles to give required tension.

ABBREVIATIONS (see also page 140)
T4L: Twist 4 left: slip next 3 sts on to cable needle and hold at the front of the work, purl next st then k 3 sts from cable needle.
T4R: Twist 4 right: slip next st on to cable needle and hold at the back of the work, k next 3 sts then p st from cable needle.
C9F: Cable 9 front: slip next 4 sts on to cable needle and hold at the front of the work, k4, p1, then k 4 sts from cable needle.
C4F: Cable 4 front: slip next 2 sts to cable needle and hold at the front of the work, knit next 2 sts then k sts from cable needle.
C4B: Cable 4 back: slip next to sts to cable needle and hold at the back of the work, knit next 2 sts then k sts from cable needle

DESIGNER PROFILE
Amanda Jones has designed knitwear since the late 1980s. She loves to use natural yarns as she feels that if you are investing your time in knitting something you should always use a yarn that will look good and last for more than one wash! She is inspired by nature and likes using textured stitches to create something interesting to knit.

1st round: Repeat set up round
2nd round: Rib as set for 31 (35:41:46) sts, (T4L, p4) twice, k4, p1, k4, (p4, T4R) x 2, p4, Rib as set to end.
This sets the position for the front cable section.

Continue to work from round 2 of the chart reading all rows from right to left until you have completed 8 rounds.

Continue to work the cable panel on reverse st st as set from 9th round.
Repeat rounds 1–16 for the pattern.

At the same time work side decrease as follows:

Next round: (1st round WS facing) *k1, k2tog tbl, pattern to 3 sts before SM, k2tog, k1 to SM; rep from * Decrease in this way on the next 2 following 10th rounds to make 97 (105:117:127) sts between front stitch markers and 86 (97:101:115) sts between back stitch markers, 183 (202:218:242) sts in total.
Work 10 rounds in pattern without shaping.

Next round: * k1, m1, pattern to 1 st before next SM, m1, k1 to SM; repeat from *.
Increase in this way on next two following 20th rounds to make 101 (109:121:131) sts for front and 93 (101:105:119) sts for back sections.

Continue without shaping until the front measures 13 in (33 cm) from beginning.
Next row: bind off 6 (6:7:7) sts, pattern to 6 (6:7:7) sts before SM, bind off 12 (12:14:14), p to 6 (6:7:7) sts before next SM, bind off 6 (6:7:7) sts.

This leaves the Front section with 89 (97:107:117) sts and the Back section with 81 (89:91:105) sts. Break yarn and leave on a holder.

LOWER SLEEVES
(make 2)
Using size 5 (3.75 mm) needles cast on 61 (61:67:69) sts.
Begin with a knit row, working in st st throughout work 20 rows.
Next row: decrease 1 st at each end of this and the

To fit sizes Small (Medium, Large, Extra Large)

21.5 (21.5:22:22.5) in (55:55:56:57) cm)

17.5:17.5:17.75:18) in (44 (44:45:46) cm)

16.5 (18.75:20.25:22.5) in (42 (47.5:51.5:57) cm)

following 2 rows to make 55 (55:61:63) sts.
Work 9 rows straight then increase 1 st at each end of the following row and every following 6th row until there are 73 (87:91:95) sts.

For 1st size only: continue to increase on every following 8th row until there are 83sts.

All sizes: continue without shaping until the work measures 17.75, (17.75, 18, 18) in, 45 (45;46:46) cm from beginning of work, ending on a WS (knit) row.
Next row: bind off 6 (6:7:7) sts at the beginning of the next 2 rows, leaving 71 (75:77:81) sts.
Break yarn and leave on a spare needle.
For 2nd sleeve do not break yarn.

Wavy pattern chart

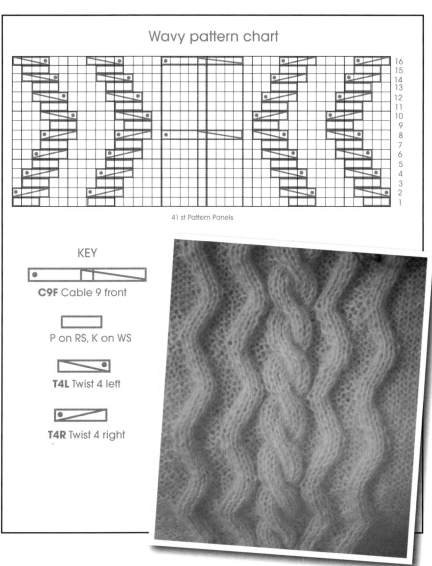

41 st Pattern Panels

KEY

C9F Cable 9 front

P on RS, K on WS

T4L Twist 4 left

T4R Twist 4 right

TOP SECTION
(worked in the round)

Joining round: with RS (purl) side of 2nd sleeve worked facing, k2, p to last 2 sts, k2 making 71 (75:77:81) sts, then with RS of body facing, starting with the front section, k2, continue in pattern as set work across front to last 2 sts, k2, being 89 (97:107:117) sts., then with RS (purl) side of sleeve facing, k2, p to last 2 sts k2 making 71 (75:77:81) sts. Finally, with RS of back section facing, k2, p to last 2 sts k2, making 81 (89:91:105) sts of back section and a total number of sts of 312 (336:352:384).

New placing of SM: Sl last 2sts (K sts) from the back section and place the SM here, now sl 2 sts back to LH needle.

Raglan shaping
NOTE: When counting the sts for each section, count Between 4-st cable pattern at each end of section.

Next round: C4F, p2tog, p to 4 sts before end of sleeve section, p2tog tbl, C4B, p2tog, pattern across front section to last 4 sts, p2tog tbl, C4F, p2tog, p across sleeve section to last 4 sts, p2tog tbl, C4B, p2tog, p across back section to last 2 sts before SM, p2tog tbl.

Make cables and decrease either side of each cable in this way on every following 4th row and continue in pattern as set until 41 (43:45:49) sts remain on the sleeve sections, 59 (65:75:85) sts remain in front section and 51 (57:59:73) sts remain in back section. Work 3 more rounds so that the decrease round will be next.

Shape sleeve head
1st decrease row: C4F, p2tog, p 16 (17:18:20), p2tog, p1, p2tog tbl, p16 (17:18:20), p2tog tbl,

C4B, p2tog, pattern across front to last 2 sts before cable, p2tog tbl, C4F, p2tog, p16 (17:18:20), p2tog, p1, p2tog tbl, p16 (17:18:20), p2tog tbl, C4B, p2tog, p across back section, end p2tog tbl. Work 3 rounds straight for 2nd, 3rd and 4th SIZES, for 1st size only see below

For first size only: decrease 1st at each end of sleeve section only on every alternate round from now on as well as the 4th row decreases.

All sizes: 2nd decrease round: C4F, p2tog, p13 (15:16:18), p2tog, p1, p2tog tbl, p13 (15:16:18), p2tog tbl. C4B, pattern across front section to 2 sts before cable, p2tog tbl, work sleeve decrease and centre decrease as before, C4F, p2tog, p across back section to last 2 sts, p2tog tbl.

Decrease in the centre of the sleeve in this way on every following 4th round until 23 (43:37:33) sts remain on sleeve section.

4th size only: continue to decrease as before every 4th row to start of neck.

1st, 2nd and 3rd sizes only: now also decrease 1 st at each end of sleeve section on every following alternate row for 2nd and 3rd sizes, continuing with this for 1st size.

Continue to decrease 1 st either side of cables on front, back and central sleeve sections on every following 4th round as set until 13 (19;19:21) sts remain in
sleeve section, 49 (53:63:71) sts in the front section and 41 (45:47:59) sts remain in back section for a total of 128 (148:160:184) sts. Work 2 rounds straight.
Neck

Change to size 3 (3.25 mm) circular needle.

Set up round for rib
1st size only: *k4, p2tog, (k3, p2) twice, k3, p2tog, k4*, p1, k3, p2tog, k3, p1, k3, p2tog, k3, (p1, k4) twice, p1, k3, p2tog, k3, p1, k3, p2tog, k3, p1; rep from * to *, p1, k3, p2tog, (k3, p1) six times, p2tog, k3, p1 making 118 sts
2nd size only: * k4, (p1, k3) x 4, p1, k4*, p1, k3, p2tog, (k3, p1) x 2, k3, p2tog, k3, (p1, k4) x 2, p1, k3, p2tog, (k3, p1) x 2, k3, p2tog, k3, p1; rep from * to *, p1, k3, p2tog, (k3, p1) x 8, k3, p2tog, k3, p1 making 142 sts
3rd size only: *k4, p1, k3, p2tog, k3, p1, k3, p2tog, k3, p1, k4*, p1, k3, p2tog, (k3, p1)x 3, k3, p2tog, k3, p1, (k4,p1)x2, k3, p2tog, (k3, p1) x3, k3, p2tog, k3, p1; rep from * to *, p1, k3, p2tog, (k3, p1) x 8, k3, p2tog, k3, p1 making 150 sts.
4th size only:* k4, p1, k3, (p2tog, k3)x3, k3, p2tog, k4*, p1, k3, p2tog, (k3, p1)x4, k3, p2tog, k3, (p1, k4)x2, p1, k3, p2tog, (k3, p1) x4, k3, p2tog, k3, p1; rep from * to *, p1, k3, p2tog, (k3, p1)x2, k3, (p2tog, k3, p1, k3)x4, p2tog, k3, p1 making 166 sts.
Continue in rib and cables as set until the rib measures 2.25ins, 6cms from beginning.
Bind off in rib.

TO FINISH

Sew in all loose ends. Join sleeve seam. Sew bind off edge of sleeve to the bind off edge of the front and back under the arms.
Press lightly.

Galway fleece

The Galway sheep is now considered to be the only "native" Irish sheep. It is difficult to be sure that any sheep is a native anymore! The result of selective breeding between Irish breeds and English Leicesters, it took over after the disappearance of its close relative the Roscommon early in the twentieth century, reaching a third of the Irish flock by 1965. Despite this, it is rare today.

Although it is classified as a "longwool" sheep, the staples from a Galway fleece are not exceptionally long and do not have the luster of other longwools; they are firm and crisp with an indistinct, fluffy crimp. Some fleeces can be used for garments worn next to the skin; others are suitable for sweaters and jackets. The fleece is all-white.

The Galway has a characteristic short neck, so that the head appears to be an extension of the long, straight back. The sheep are hornless, with a top-knot, and wool down to the knees. They are similar in appearance to the Romney, particularly around the head and ears.

The adult sheep are medium-sized, with the ewes weighing around 163 lbs (74 kg) and the rams 176 lbs (80 kg) on average. Galway ewes are long-lived, lambing successfully up to the age of ten and, with good husbandry, are able to produce and rear twins.

Most Galways are farmed in Ireland. Due to competition from imported breeds, the number of registered ewes fell from around 700 in 37 flocks in 1965, to only just over 100 in 10 flocks by 1993. But this is now recovering and there were nearly 870 sheep in 40 flocks by 2007. This would qualify the breed for Vulnerable status under the UK's Rare Breeds Survival Trust criteria. It has gained the Galway breed recognition and protection at Irish national level as part of the country's Rural Environment Protection Scheme.

There are a few flocks in the UK but none are reported in the U.S.

BREED AT A GLANCE

Sheep type: Longwool.
Appearance: White and hornless.
Rare breeds status: Listed as Vulnerable in Ireland, a conservation breed in the U.S., on the UK Rare Breeds Survival Trust watchlist.
Further information: Irish breed society: www.galwaysheep.ie. Galway Sheep Breeders Society of Great Britain: www.sheep.ukf.net.
History: A variant of the now extinct Roscommon breed which it succeeded thanks to it being faster growing (and therefore more commercial), finer, and heavier.

clean fleece

Aran yarn

FLEECE FACT FILE
Fleece weight: 5.5–7.7 lbs (2.5–3.5 kg)
Staple length: 4.5–5.5 in (11.5–14 cm)
Micron count: Around 30-plus
Crimp: Indistinct wavy
Handle: Crisp
Natural colors: True white (not cream)
Mixed colors: None
Luster: None

raw fleece

Close-up of white Aran knitted sample

carded fleece

Galway yarn

The clean, white Galway is a great, do-it-all fiber. It crosses the boundaries between lustrous longwools and mid-range or Downland wools. In general it makes softer yarns than the wool produced by the more numerous Lleyn, with good definition. It deserves to be more widely used.

The fleece of the Galway sheep is of a medium length, with a soft, fluffy, and indistinct crimp. The staples are long enough for worsted spinning.

Worsted-spun Galway yarn gives good stitch definition when knitted, and so Galway yarn is a good candidate for textured knits such as Guernseys. It is also ideal for traditional Aran-style textured pullovers. The Aran Islands are off the coast of Ireland, in the Galway Bay, and so the knitting developed there would surely be related to the native fleeces!

The wool is mid-range in fineness, nor is it the softest available (although some fleeces yield wool soft enough to be worn next to the skin), but it is hard-wearing. It does not felt well. Thus, the stitches in a textured pattern remain distinct after years of wear. When dyed, Galway wool has a clear, strong color.

I have chosen a modern take on an Aran sweater design for this Galway pattern. Other options would include the patterns in Gotland or Cotswold yarn, which will have a more textured result. You could also try the Jacob, North Ronaldsay, Ryeland, and Zwartbles patterns, or the bag in Hebridean yarn.

When knitted, Galway yarn gives great stitch definition in cable designs as well as between knit and purl stitches—adding texture to the simplest knitted fabric.

YARN USER'S GUIDE

Good for ...
- Inner and outer garments, depending on the fleece
- Textured stitches
- Dyeing

Not so good for ...
- Felting
- Baby clothes

Pucker cable tunic

By Amanda Crawford

This attractive all-over cable tunic has a puckered cable design created by cabling on fewer, and then more, stitches in the cable panels. It has drop shoulders and hangs straight from the shoulders. The relaxed feel is enhanced by the turned-back ribbed cuffs and a grown-on funnel neck—a simple rib roll-neck may be substituted to match the cuffs, if desired. It is ideal for a "big" look, and pairs well with leggings and boots, or when worn casually with jeans. It can also be made longer to create a tunic dress, or adapted, using either neck design, with a rib welt and shorter cuffs for a man's outdoor pullover.

DESIGNER PROFILE

Amanda Crawford works almost exclusively with natural wool. She designed knitwear for major stores before deciding to follow her passion for hand-knitting. Today she designs for magazines.

YARN REQUIREMENTS

Pure Galway Wool Aran yarn

• Total amount of wool by weight and approximate length

U.S. size 4: 900 g / 1,368 yds (1,260 m)
U.S. size 6: 900 g / 1,368 yds (1,260 m)
U.S. size 8: 1,000 g / 1,520 yds (1,400 m)
U.S. size 10: 1,000 g / 1,520 yds (1,400 m)
U.S. size 12: 1,100 g / 1,672 yds (1,540 m)
U.S. size 14: 1,100 g / 1,672 yds (1,540 m)
U.S. size 16: 1,200 g / 1,824 yds (1,680 m)
U.S. size 18: 1,200 g / 1,824 yds (1,680 m)

Method

BACK and FRONT
(make two, both alike)

Using size 8 (5mm) needles cast on 105 (109, 115, 121, 129, 135, 141, 145) sts.

Foundation rows:
U.S. Sizes 4, 6, 8, 10 and 18 only
Row A (RS): p2 (4, 7, 10, -, -, -, 1), *k8, sl 1, k8, p4, rep from * to last 19 (21, 24, 27, -, -, -, 18) sts, k8, sl 1, k8, p2 (4, 7, 10, -, -, -, 1).
Row B: k2 (4, 7, 10, -, -, -, 1), *p17, k4, rep from * to last 19 (21, 24, 27, -, -, -, 18) sts, p17, k2 (4, 7, 10, -, -, -, 1).

U.S. Sizes 12, 14 and 16 only
Row A (RS): P- (-, -, -, 1, 4, 7, -), sl 1, k8, p4, *k8, sl 1, k8, p4, rep from * to last - (-, -, -, 10, 13, 16, -) sts, k8, sl 1, P- (-, -, -, 1, 4, 7, -).
Row B: K- (-, -, -, 1, 4, 7, -), p9, k4, *p17, k4, rep from * to last - (-, -, -, 10, 13, 16, -) sts, p9, k - (-, -, -, 1, 4, 7, -).

Continue in pattern:
U.S. Sizes 4, 6, 8, 10 and 18 only
Row 1 (RS): P2 (4, 7, 10, -, -, -, 1), *k8, sl 1, k8, p4, rep from * to last 19 (21, 24, 27, -, -, -, 18) sts, k8, sl 1, k8, p2 (4, 7, 10, -, -, -, 1).
Row 2 and all alternate rows: K2 (4, 7, 10, -, -, -, 1), *p17, K4, rep from * to last 19 (21, 24, 27, -, -, -, 18) sts, p17, k2 (4, 7, 10, -, -, -, 1).
Row 3 (RS): As row 1.
Row 5 (RS): P2 (4, 7, 10, -, -, -, 1), *CB8, sl 1, CF8, p4, rep from * to last 19 (21, 24, 27, -, -, -, 18) sts, k8, sl 1, k8, p2 (4, 7, 10, -, -, -, 1).
Row 7 (RS): As row 1.
Row 9 (RS): P2 (4, 7, 10, -, -, -, 1), *k2, CB6, sl 1, CF6, k2, p4, rep from * to last 19 (21, 24, 27, -, -, -, 18) sts, k2, CB6, sl 1, CB6, k2, p2 (4, 7, 10, -, -, -, 1).
Row 11 (RS): As row 1.
Row 13 (RS): P2 (4, 7, 10, -, -, -, 1), *k4, CB4, sl 1, CF4, k4, p4, rep from * to last 19 (21, 24, 27, -, -, -,

18) sts, k4, CB4, sl 1, CB4, K4, p2 (4, 7, 10, -, -, -, 1).
Row 14: As row 2.
These 14 rows set pattern.
Continue straight in pattern until work measures 21 (21, 22, 22, -, -, -, 24.5) in (53 (53, 56, 56, -, -, -, 62) cm), ending with RS facing.

Continue in pattern:
U.S. Sizes 12, 14 and 16 only
Row 1 (RS): P- (-, -, -, 1, 4, 7, -), sl 1, k8, p4, *k8, sl 1, k8, p4, rep from * to last - (-, -, -, 10, 13, 16, -) sts, k8, sl 1, P- (-, -, -, 1, 4, 7, -).
Row 2 and all alternate rows: K- (-, -, -, 1, 4, 7, -), p9, k4, *p17, k4, repeat from * to last -(-, -, -, 10, 13, 16, -) sts, p9, k- (-, -, -, 1, 4, 7, -).
Row 3 (RS): As row 1.
Row 5 (RS): P- (-, -, -, 1, 4, 7, -), sl 1, CF8, p4, *CB8, sl 1, CF8, p4, rep from * to last - (-, -, -, 10, 13, 16, -) sts, CB8, sl 1, p-(-, -, -, 1, 4, 7, -).
Row 7 (RS): As row 1.
Row 9 (RS): P- (-, -, -, 1, 4, 7, -), sl

MEASUREMENTS
Bust size: 32 (34, 36, 38, 40, 42, 44, 46) in (82 (86, 90, 96, 102, 107, 112, 117) cm)
Garment size: 36.5 (38, 39.5, 42, 44, 46, 48, 49.5) in (92 (96, 100, 106, 112, 118, 122, 126) cm)
Length: 21.5 (21.5, 23, 23, 24, 24, 25, 25) in (55 (55, 58, 58, 61, 61, 64, 64) cm)
Instructions are given for the smallest size first, followed by the larger sizes in brackets.

NEEDLES & NOTIONS
A pair needles size 8 (5mm)
A pair size 8 (5mm) circular needles
Cable needle

GAUGE
Approx 23 sts x 25.5 rows = 4 in (10 cm) over cable pattern on size 8 (5 mm) needles
Adjust needle size to give required tension

ABBREVIATIONS (see also page 140)
CB8 (6, 4) = slip next 4 (3, 2) sts on to a cable needle and hold at back of work. K next 4 (3, 2) sts then k sts from cable needle.
CF8 (6, 4) = slip next 4 (3, 2) sts on to a cable needle and hold at front of work. K next 4 (3, 2) sts then k sts from cable needle.
Sl 1 = slip one stitch with yarn held at back of work (including after purl stitches)

SKILL LEVEL

1, k2, CF6, p4, *k2, CB6, sl 1, CF6, k2, p4, rep from * to last - (-, -, -, 10, 13, 16, -) sts, k2, CB6, sl 1, p- (-, -, -, 1, 4, 7, -).

Row 11 (RS): As row 1.
Row 13 (RS): P- (-, -, -, 1, 4, 7, -), sl 1, k4, CF4, p4, *k4, CB4, sl 1, CF4, k4, p4, rep from * to last -(-, -, -, 10, 13, 16, -) sts, k4, CB4, sl 1, p- (-, -, -, 1, 4, 7, -).
Row 14: As row 2.
These 14 rows set pattern, continue straight in pattern until work measures - (-, -, -, 23¼, 23¼, 24½, -) in (- (-, -, -, 59, 59, 62, -) cm), ending with RS facing.

Shape Shoulders
All sizes
Keeping pattern correct, bind/cast off 10 (11, 11, 12, 13, 14, 15, 16) sts at beginning of next 2 rows, 10 (10, 11, 12, 13, 14, 15, 15) sts at beginning of following 2 rows and 9 (10, 11, 12, 13, 14, 14, 15) sts at beginning of next 2 rows, leaving 47 (47, 49, 49, 51, 51, 53, 53) sts.
Leave remaining 47 (47, 49, 49, 51, 51, 53, 53) sts on a stitch holder.

SLEEVES
(make two)
Using size 8 (5mm) needles cast on 74 (74, 79, 79, 84, 84, 84, 84) sts.
Row 1: (RS): P3 *k3, p2, rep from

* to last 6 sts, k3, p3.
Row 2: K3 *p3, k2, rep from * to last 6 sts, p3, k3.
These 2 rows set rib, continue straight in rib for 8 in (20 cm) ending with WS row facing for next row. Repeat row 2, increasing 3 (3, 2, 2, 3, 3, 3, 3) sts evenly across row. 77 (77, 81, 81, 87, 87, 87, 87) sts.

Cont in pattern:
Row 1 (RS): p2, K3 (3, 5, 5, 8, 8, 8, 8), p4 *k8, sl 1, k8, p4, rep from * to last 5 (5, 7, 7, 10, 10, 10, 10) sts, K3 (3, 5, 5, 8, 8, 8, 8), p2.
Row 2 and every following alternate row: k2, P3 (3, 5, 5, 8, 8, 8, 8), K4, *p17, k4, repeat from * to last 5 (5, 7, 7, 10, 10, 10, 10) sts, p3 (3, 5, 5, 8, 8, 8, 8), k2.
Continue with rows 3-14 in pucker cable pattern as placed, increasing 1st each end of next row and every following 4th row 2 sts in from edge and taking extra sts into pattern until 109 (109, 115, 115, 121, 121, 127, 127) sts.
P first and last 2 sts to give a

neat edge for sewing up. Continue straight in pattern until sleeve measures 19.5 (19.5, 19.5, 19.5, 20.5, 20.5, 21.25, 21.25) in (50 (50, 50, 50, 52, 52, 54, 54) cm) ending with RS facing for next row.
Bind/Cast off.

FINISHING
Press work carefully.
Join shoulder seams.

NECK TRIM
Using size 8 (5mm) circular needle transfer sts from stitch holders. 94 (94, 98, 98, 102, 102, 106, 106) sts.

Keeping pattern as set continue straight for 3 in (8cm), or longer if desired, ending with RS facing for next row.
Bind/Cast off.

Sew side seams and underarm together as one continuous seam, remembering to reverse the seam for the first 4.75 in (12 cm) of the cuff as this will be turned back.

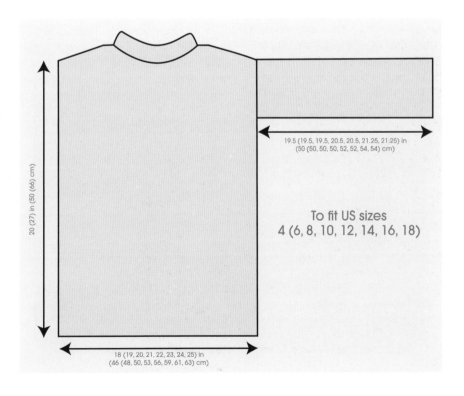

20 (27) in (50 (66) cm)

19.5 (19.5, 19.5, 20.5, 20.5, 21.25, 21.25) in (50 (50, 50, 50, 52, 52, 54, 54) cm)

To fit US sizes
4 (6, 8, 10, 12, 14, 16, 18)

18 (19, 20, 21, 22, 23, 24, 25) in (46 (48, 50, 53, 56, 59, 61, 63) cm)

Gotland fleece

As a Gotland owner of many years I am biased—I consider this to be an extremely intelligent sheep, with a sense of humor and mischief. Today's Gotland is an improved version of the original breed, with a more consistent fleece and conformation. Although they no longer have horns, they have distinct horn craters, and some develop mini vestigial horns or scurs.

The longwool fleece of the Gotland sheep is soft enough to be worn next to the skin. The texture is so light it can be similar to that of a fine mohair.

The characteristics of an individual fleece will depend on the strain of the breed, but they are always long, lustrous and with a wavy —even curly—crimp.

Gotlands, particularly the rams, may have a dark mane of coarse hair at the neck. The lambs are born black, and this color remains on the hairless legs and heads. The skin is naturally gray in color, but some sheep have one or more white socks, white around the eyes, or white blazes on the face.

The Gotland is sometimes known as the three-crop sheep as it is good for fleece, skins, and meat. It was first imported into the UK in the 1970s, and to the U.S. in 2003. It is also farmed in Australia, Sweden, Holland, and Denmark.

The adult sheep are small, the ewes growing to 121–154 lbs (55–70 kg) and the rams to 165–187 lbs (75–85 kg). Like other primitive sheep breeds they are hardy animals. Although not numerous in the UK, with around 200 registered breeding ewes, they are becoming increasingly popular.

In New Zealand, the famous Stansborough flock produced the wool used for the cloaks worn by the Hobbits in *The Lord of the Rings* films.

BREED AT A GLANCE

Sheep type: Primitive, northern short-tailed.
Appearance: Gray—sometimes with white markings—black heads, and legs; no horns.
Rare breeds status: None.
Further information: UK breed society: www.gotlandsheep.com.
North American and U.S. breed societies: www.americangotlandsheep.com and www.gsbana.org.
History: From the island of Gotland, off the coast of Sweden, where they were known as gute sheep. The breed was originally developed for its skin; this may have begun in the time of the Vikings.

dark gray
4-ply yarn

dark gray DK
yarn

dark gray denim
over-dyed DK yarn

mid-gray slate over-
dyed 4-ply yarn

raw fleece

FLEECE FACT FILE
Fleece weight: 2–8 lbs (1–4 kg)
Staple length: 10 in (25 cm)
Micron count: 28–32, but can be well
below this for lambs and selected
adults, as low as 20 in some cases
Crimp: Well developed and wavy
Handle: Soft and supple
Natural colors: Shades of gray
(from pale to charcoal); some white
and brown
Mixed colors: Grays and brownish gray
Luster: High

carded mid-gray
fleece

carded pale
fleece

Close-up of dark gray DK knitted sample

mid-gray DK yarn

scoured
fleece

carded dark-gray
fleece

pale DK yarn

Gotland yarn

Gotland wool is very soft and fine, with various shades of gray from silver to charcoal. Among sheep, Gotlands probably produce a fleece most like mohair in texture. It has a distinct lock formation, with a neat, tiny crimp in lambs, which lengthens out into wavy ringlets as they grow older.

Make the most of the many shades of wool available from a Gotland fleece to create naturally multicolored garments. The result will be a soft, silky garment that drapes well.

their way free of the yarn. As a result it is better semi-worsted or woollen-spun, which results in a lean, stylish but slightly fluffy yarn. Hand-spinners will find Gotland quite a challenging task.

Gotland may sometimes feel hard when newly spun as it responds less well to twisting than some fibers, but it softens beautifully with age.

Gotland can be spun fine for lace work or thick for chunky sweaters, but the propensity to felt will mean that over time a textured Aran or Guernsey design will gradually lose its crisply distinct details, although it will also become warmer and more windproof.

Gotland yarn can happily be used as a substitute to knit the patterns designed for Cotswold and Wensleydale

YARN USER'S GUIDE

Good for ...
• Knitting
• Crochet
• Spinning
• Weaving
• Felting
• Dyeing

Not so good for ...
• Textured knitting

yarns in this book. It can also be used for the patterns designed for Jacob wool, or the Shetland lacy scarf, where it will achieve a different, more draped style.

The fleece will grow up to 12 in (30 cm), but farmers rarely allow this because it felts very easily and, if left on the animal for a year, the beautiful individual locks will become matted and impossible to separate for spinning (although the matted fleece makes an ideal pet bed or home insulation). To prevent this Gotlands are shorn twice a year to produce fleece with a staple length of 4–6 in (10–15 cm). Like most sheep and goats, Gotlands can produce coarser wool with age, including straighter hairs, kemp, and less crimp.

As a luster longwool, Gotland dyes wonderfully, and the over-dyeing of the natural silvers and grays produces very attractive shades, particularly when using pinks, blues, and purples, but also in greens, rusts, and golds.

Although Gotland wool can be worsted-spun to enhance its luster, it may then shed or pill as the smooth hairs gently work

Long cardigan with hand-warmer pockets

By Myra Mortlock and Sue Blacker

This cardigan has a deep welt, which can be left unsewn with side slits for a more relaxed fit or sewn together. Using size 7 (4.5 mm) needles for the whole body will leave the welt looser, which is probably more flattering for this length, but we suggest you use size 6 (4 mm) or even size 5 (3.75 mm) needles for the collar to make it stiffer. The buttons are optional. The deep shawl collar can be made in one color or with a contrast lining. A multi-cable motif decorates the center-back. Hand-warmer pockets add extra warmth.

The sleeves are worked downwards with two options: either a tight, long cuff in two and two rib to match the front bands (worked on size 6 (4 mm) needles) or doubled offset rib cuffs to match the collar and which make the garment suitable to wear as a jacket or coat. If making the tight cuff, the sleeves can be worked on circular and double-pointed needles; the offset rib version works best on two needles.

We have used Gotland DK yarn, but any other DK yarn would be suitable.

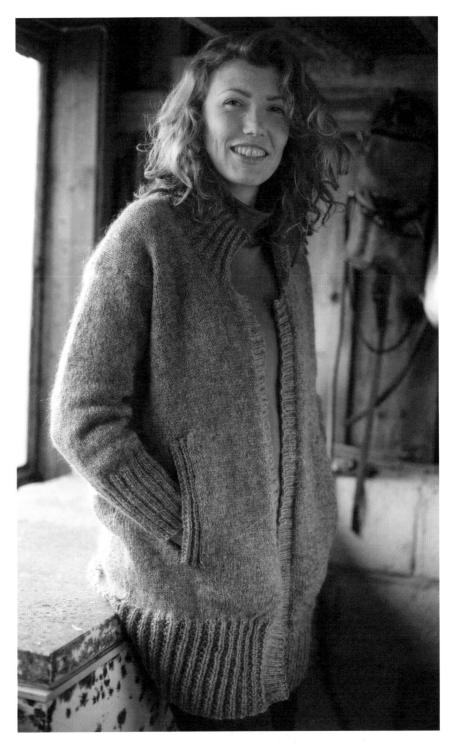

YARN REQUIREMENTS

Gotland worsted-weight Double Knitting yarn
• Total amount of wool by weight and approximate length:
Small: 750 g / 1,785 yds (1,650 m)
Medium: 800 g / 1,904 yds (1,760 m)
Large: 850 g / 2,023 yds (1,870 m)

Method

BACK (make one)

Using size 6 (4 mm) needles (or size 7 (4.5 mm) for looser welt), cast on 109 (117, 125) sts.
Row 1: K2, p2 to last st, k1.
Row 2: as row 1.
Repeat until work measures 6 in (15 cm) for all sizes. Change to size 7 (4.5 mm) needles and knit one row, increasing 1 st in center of row to give 110 (118, 126) sts. Continue in stocking stitch until work measures 23 in (58 cm) from cast-on edge.

Shape armhole
Tip: to get a smooth curve, slip the first st in all these bind off rows.
Bind off 5 sts at start of next 2 rows, 4 sts at start of following 2 rows, 3 sts next 2 rows, 2 sts following 2 rows and 1 st next 2 rows. Total decrease 15 sts on each side.

Center motif in 3 sections
Section 1:
RS facing, mark center 34 sts for cable motif (30 sts with border of 2 reverse stocking st each side).
Begin pattern as follows:
RS facing, k 23 (27, 31) sts, p2, T3, p2, T3, p2, T3, p4, T3, p2, T3, p2, T3, p2, K to end.

MEASUREMENTS
Size Small (US 8-10)
Medium (US 12-14)
Large (US 16-18)
The garment is designed as outerwear and to be quite loose-fitting, so the medium size comes up at 44 in (112 cm) around the bust, 31 in (79 cm) from neck to hem, and 23 in (58.5 cm) from the under arm to the hem. The sleeves are 17 in (43 cm) long.
NOTE: to shorten the cardigan, reduce length of body by 1 in (2.5 cm) below and above the pockets. To re-size it to make it slightly smaller or larger, use one size smaller or larger needles. Instructions are given for the smallest size first, followed by medium and large in brackets.

NEEDLES & NOTIONS
One pair each of needles size 5 (3.75 mm), 6 (4 mm) and 7 (4.5 mm)
Stitch markers or colored thread
Stitch holder
7 buttons (optional)

GAUGE
Approx 21 sts x 22 rows = 4 in (10 cm) over stocking stitch on size 7 (4.5 mm) needles
Adjust needle size to give required tension.

ABBREVIATIONS (see also page 140)
Offset 2 x 2 rib: (see instructions below, k2, p2 all rows).
2 x 2 rib (for front bands): Row 1: (k2, p2) repeat to end. Row 2: (p2, k2) repeat to end.
T3 (twist 3): slip next 2 sts onto cable needle and hold at back of work, knit next st then knit 2 sts from cable needle.
T5L (twist 5 left): slip next 3 sts onto cable needle and hold at front of work, purl next 2 sts from left-hand needle, then knit sts from cable needle.
T5R (twist 5 right): slip next 2 sts onto cable needle and hold at back of work, knit next 3 sts from left-hand needle, then purl sts from cable needle.
C6F (cable 6 front): slip next 3 sts onto cable needle and hold at front of work, knit next 3 sts from left-hand needle, then knit sts from cable needle.
C6B (cable 6 back): slip next 3 sts onto cable needle and hold at back of work, knit next 3 sts from left-hand needle, then knit sts from cable needle.

Next row: work all sts as they present themselves.
Continue, repeating these 2 rows until 14 rows of pattern have been worked.

Section 2:
Work cable design over 14 rows as follows:

Row 1: K 23 (27, 31) p2 (T5L) 3 times. (T5R) 3 times p2, k 23 (27, 31).
Row 2: P 23 (27, 31) k4, p3, k2, p3, k2, p6, k2, p3, k2, p3, k4, p23 (27, 31).
Row 3: K 23 (27, 31) p4, (T5L) twice, C6B, (T5R) twice, p4, k to end.

Row 4: P 23 (27, 31) k6, p3, k2, p12, k2, p3, k6, p to end.
Instructions following are for the center panel of 34 sts only.
Row 5: P6, T5L, (C6F) twice, T5R, p6.
Row 6: K8, p18, k8.
Row 7: P8, (C6B) 3 times, p8.
Row 8: K8, p18, k8.
Row 9: P6, T5R, (C6F) twice, T5L, p6.
Row 10: as row 4.
Row 11: P4, (T5R) twice, C6B, (T5L) twice, p4.
Row 12: as row 2.
Row 13: P2, (T5R) 3 times (T5L) 3 times, p2.
Row 14: K2, (p3, k2) twice, p3, k4, p3, (k2, p3) twice, k2.

Section 3:
Repeat section 1 working 13 rows. End with RS row.
Work 9 (11, 13) rows stocking stitch to shoulder.

Shape shoulder
RS facing, knit 28 (32, 36) sts and turn. Leave remaining sts on hold (they can stay on needle).

Row 1: at neck edge, slip 1 purlwise, p1, psso purl to end.
Row 2: knit without shaping.
Repeat row 1.
At shoulder edge, bind off 8 (9, 10) sts.
At neck edge, slip 1 purlwise, p1, psso as before.
Repeat these 2 rows.
Decrease once more at neck edge then bind off all remaining shoulder sts.
Leaving 24 (24, 24) sts on holder for back of neck, make second shoulder reversing all shaping.

RIGHT FRONT
(make one)
Using size 6 (4 mm) needles (or size 7 (4.5 mm) for looser welt), cast on 55 (59, 63) sts.
Work in offset 2x2 rib, K2, P2 to last 3 sts, K2, P1 to same length as back.
Change to size 7 (4.5 mm) needles and st st and work 24 rows.
Divide for pocket opening.
RS facing, k 30 sts and turn,

leaving remaining 29 sts on hold. WS facing, cast on 11 sts. Slip 1, k1, p2, k2, p2, k2, p1 and purl to end.
Next row RS facing, knit 30 sts. (k2, p2) repeat once, k2, p1. Continue working offset 2x2 rib at pocket opening until 52 pocket rows have been worked. Turn and bind off 11 sts, break off yarn leaving a length of about 12 in (30 cm) at the pocket edge and place remaining 30 sts on hold.

Make pocket lining: cast on 30 sts. Work 23 rows in st st. At end of 23rd row (RS until facing) knit on the sts held for front and continue in st st for 30 rows.
Tip: it may be easier to pin or tack the pocket lining in place at this stage

Bind off 3 sts at pocket edge on next and following 9 alternate rows (30 sts in total)
Tip: slip first of bind off sts through back of loop each time to get a smooth edge.
WS facing, work 25, 29, 33 sts. Continue to work across the 30 sts on hold with main yarn joining the two sections together. Tack pocket and edge in place with contrast thread (to unpick and press before final sewing).

Continue until front measures same as back to armhole (23 in (58 cm) or required length). Work armhole shaping as for Back. Then bind off 1 more st at armhole edge (39, 43, 47 sts remaining). Continue until right front measures 26 in (67 cm).

Shape neck: bind off at neck edge 5, 4, 3, 2, 1 sts on alternate rows (24, 28, 32 sts remaining, which is (2, 1, 1) sts more than the back shoulder shaping). Continue until front measures same as back to shoulder. Bind off over 3 alternate rows to match back shaping.

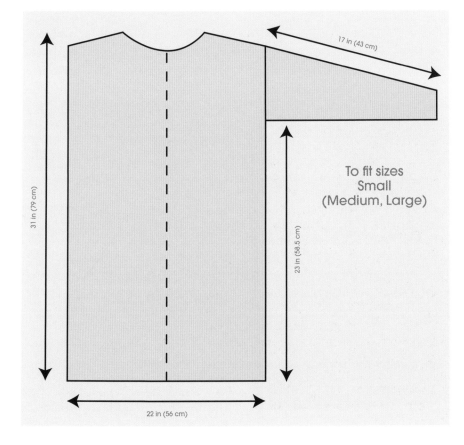

17 in (43 cm)

To fit sizes
Small
(Medium, Large)

31 in (79 cm)

23 in (58.5 cm)

22 in (56 cm)

LEFT FRONT
(make one)

Work as right front to pocket opening.

RS facing, knit 25 29, 33 sts. Cast on 11 into next st for pocket edge

NOTE: to get an exact match at the pocket edge this side is worked as follows, starting with the cast on sts.

Row 1: s1, p1, k2, p2, k2, p2, k1, k to end.

Row 2: p 30 sts, k2, p2, k2, p2, k2, p1

Continue working offset 2x2 rib at pocket opening until 52 pocket rows have been worked. Place these sts on a spare needle or holder.

Make pocket lining. Cast on 30 sts. **Starting with a purl row**, work 24 rows.

Next row: WS facing, purl across pocket lining and continue across 25, 29, 33 held sts.

Continue to match right front reversing all shapings.

SLEEVES
(make two)

Join shoulder seam. With size 6 (4 mm) needles and right side facing, pick up and knit 123 sts from armhole edge. Change to size 7 (4.5 mm) needles and work in stocking stitch.

Row 1 (with right side facing)**:** K2tog, k1, (k2tog, k2) 5 times, k28 (k2tog, k2) 5 times, k28, (k2tog, k2) 6 times. 106 sts.

Row 2 and all alternate rows: purl if using two needles, or knit if using a circular needle.

Row 3: (k2, k2tog) 3 times. k37, (k2tog) 3 times, k39 (k2tog,k2) 3 times. 97 sts.

Row 5: Knit

Row 7: K2, (k2tog,k1) 3 times. K to last 10 sts,

(k2tog, k1) 3 times, k1. 91 sts.

Row 9: Knit.

Row 11: K2, (k2tog) 3 times, k to the last 8 sts, (k2tog) 3 times, k2. 85 sts.

Row 13: Knit.

Row 15: K2, k2tog, k to last 4 sts, k2tog, k2. 83 sts.

Continue to decrease 1 st at each end of every following 6th row as set until 63 sts are left on needle.

Work 4 more rows (or adjust length here).

If making the tight cuff change to size 6 (4 mm) needles, and decrease 3 sts evenly on first row working in k2, p2rib for 5 in (13 cm). Bind off in rib.

If working the looser cuff in off-set rib, change to size 6 (4 mm) needles and work in rib for 10 in (26 cm), if using one color, or 5 in (13 cm) in main color and 5 in (13 cm) in contrast color. Bind off in rib.

NOTE: work the offset rib as follows:

Row 1: SL1, *k2, p2*, repeat from * to * to last 4 sts, k2, p1, k1

All subsequent rows: as row 1

Please remember when picking up stitches that this design works for multiples of 4 sts plus 1 only.

COLLAR (make one)

Using size 6 (4 mm) needles and with RS facing pick up 41 (43, 45) sts between center front and shoulder, 8 (9, 10) sts at side of back neck, 24 sts from holder (pick up 2 of these as one st to make the offset rib work with an uneven number of sts), 8 (9, 10) to shoulder and 41 (43, 45) to center front. Work offset rib for 4 in (10 cm). Change to contrast color if used, work 4 in (10 cm). Bind off firmly in rib.

CENTER BANDS
(make two)

Pick up 120 sts between bottom of welt and half way up on collar on each of the fronts. Add/reduce number of sts if length of garment has been increased/reduced.

For buttonhole band: *K2, P2* repeat to end. Work 4 rows. Work 7 buttonholes to fit your chosen buttons, evenly spaced along next row. Continue until 9 rows have been worked. Bind/ Bind off in rib.

For button band: row 1 *P2, K2* repeat to end. Check bands to make sure that rib pattern is knitted evenly and will meet correctly with buttonhole side. Work to 9 rows. Bind off in rib.

MAKING UP

Turn down collar onto wrong side, pin in place matching pattern. Sew down firmly. Neaten ends. With contrast wool, tack the buttonhole band into place over the button band to match exactly and sew on buttons at buttonholes (do this after washing and pressing the garment to be more certain of a perfect match). Sew up side seams (leaving slits at the bottom welt if desired). If wide cuffs have been made, turn under off-set rib cuff and stitch in place. Sew seams.

Fall leaves beret

By Rita Taylor

This attractive beret is made with dyed Gotland Double Knitting yarn and has a lacy, leaf-shaped motif, with twelve leaves falling from the crown to the brim.

It is made in one size and is reasonably stretchy, but if you need to alter it slightly, use one size larger or smaller knitting needles. If you need to alter it by more than this, increase or decrease in multiples of eight stitches to accommodate the design.

The worsted-weight DK yarn is used doubled throughout. Use one color, or two closely toned shades, or the lace pattern will be lost. This is a great starting point for first-time lace knitters.

DESIGNER PROFILE

Rita Taylor has been a keen knitter since childhood and is interested in traditonal Scottish patterns. She recreates ganseys for the British Knitting & Crochet Guild.

YARN REQUIREMENTS

Gotland worsted-weight DK yarn
• Total amount of wool by weight and approximate length:
100 g/238 yds (220 m)
• Use yarn doubled throughout

Method

Using size 5 (3.75 mm) needles, cast on 101 sts.
Work in p3 k1 rib, beginning first row with p2, until work measures 2 in (5 cm) from cast on edge. Change to size 8 (5 mm) needles and continue for a further 2 in (5 cm).

Start pattern:
Row 1: P2 (yf, k1, yrn, p2) to end.
Row 2: K2 (p3, k2) to end.
Row 3: P2 (k1, yf, k1, yf, p3tog) to last 2 sts, p2.
Row 4: K4 (p5, k1) to last 4, k4.
Row 5: P4 (k2, yf, k1, yf, k2, p5) to last 4, p4.
Row 6: K4 (p7, k5) to end.
Row 7: P4 (k3, yf, k1, yf, k3, p5) to end.
Row 8: K4 (p9, k5) to end.
Row 9: P4 (k9, p5) to end.
Row 10: as row 8.
Row 11: as row 9.
Row 12: as row 8.
Row 13: P4 (ssk, k5, k2tog, p5) to end.
Row 14: as row 6.
Row 15: P4 (ssk, k3, k2tog, p5) to end.
Row 16: K4 (p5, k5) to last 4, k4.
Row 17: P4 (ssk, k1, k2tog, p5) to end.
Row 18: K4 (p3, k5) to end.
Row 19: P1, p2tog (p1, sl1, k2tog, psso) to last 4, p1, p2tog, p1.
Row 20: K1, ssk (p1, k1) to last 3, k2tog, k1.
Row 21: K1, p1 to last st, k1.
Row 22: P1, k1 to last st, p1.
Row 23: K1, p3tog, to last st, k1.
Row 24: P1, k1 to last st, p1.
Row 25: K1 (p1, sl1 k2tog, psso) to end.
Break off wool leaving a tail of about 16 in (40 cm). Thread wool through remaining sts, draw up and fasten off. Use remaining wool to sew back seam.

MEASUREMENTS
One size to fit an average adult head (21 in (53 cm) approx)

NEEDLES & NOTIONS
One pair size 5 (3.75 mm) and size 8 (5 mm) needles

GAUGE
Approx 20 sts x 24 rows = 4 in (10 cm) using doubled yarn over stocking stitch on size 8 (5 mm) needles
Adjust needle size to give required tension.

ABBREVIATIONS (see also page 140)
ssk: (slip, slip, knit) slip 2 stitches knitwise from the left to the right needle, then insert the tip of the left needle into the fronts of the slipped stitches and knit them together from this position.
yf: wrap the yarn over the needle, to create an extra stitch on the return row and a small lace hole (knit stitches).
yrn: bring yarn forward, take over the needle and then back to the front of the work again, to create an extra stitch on the return row and a small lace hole (purl stitches).

SKILL LEVEL

Hebridean fleece

The hardy Hebridean sheep is gaining a special place in British conservation grazing, as it manages with very little human intervention, including producing one or two lambs each year. It is probably not a true native: the black genes appear to have come from the Middle East and managed to reach northern Europe over the centuries as merchants traveled and traded livestock.

The fleece of the Hebridean sheep is completely black, but gradually gains gray hairs with age, so that it is possible to make gray yarns and weave them into striped rug designs. It may also be bleached brown by the sun. The type of fleece varies: some are soft and fine, others are more dense.

Originally, most small, native Scottish sheep were northern short-tailed breeds with brown faces. They were descended from Iron Age breeds, and known as Dunface sheep. Being small, they became minorities on the highlands and were eventually found only on the islands. The modern sheep dates from the ninth century.

Small parkland sheep such as the Hebridean have not proved to be commercially viable for meat or wool and used to rely on hobby farmers for their existence. Recently, ewes have been cross-bred for better meat production. The meat is recognized as lean, healthy, and tasty. If bred with rams with white genes, the lambs are white, which results in more profitable wool production. Ewes grow to 77–88 lbs (35–40 kg) and rams to 110–121 lbs (50–55 kg).

When intensive farming developed after 1945 Hebridean numbers fell. By 1973, it was designated "rare" by the Rare Breeds Survival Trust. However, its success at conservation grazing means it no longer requires preservation, and is now listed as a Native Breed. No flocks are recorded in the U.S.

BREED AT A GLANCE

Sheep type: Primitive, northern short-tailed.
Appearance: Small, with black fleece and imposing horns (a few have four but some ewes have none).
Rare breeds status: Native breed not on the UK at-risk register.
Further information: UK breed society: www.hebrideansheep.org.uk.
History: Descended from a flock of wild native sheep taken from the island of Uist in the 1880s and selected and bred as black for parkland grazing in Cumbria.

scoured
fleece

carded fleece

FLEECE FACT FILE
Fleece weight: 2.2–4.4 lb (1–2 kg)
Staple length: 2–6 in (5–15 cm)
Micron count: 35 plus
Crimp: Generally low
Handle: Ranges from dense and coarse to fine and soft
Natural colors: Black, sometimes very dark brown; may be bleached brown by the sun or turn gray with age
Mixed colors: None
Luster: Minimal

Close-up of pure Aran knitted sample

raw fleece

Aran yarn

Hebridean yarn

Hebridean wool is often a dull black in color, without much luster. Once it begins to gray with age, or to be bleached by the sun, it can be quite a flat off-black bitter chocolate color, with plenty of kempy fibers.

Wool from a Hebridean lamb or shearling is softer and slightly lustrous when compared with that of an adult sheep. If this is not available, an older fleece can be improved by blending it with mohair to produce a lovely soft and shiny charcoal color, or with Manx Loagthan to provide a rich chocolate brown with great depth. I often use Hebridean wool to add a little color and texture to the smoother and blander Corriedale or Falkland wools.

However, the fleeces can be matted or contain vegetation, which can be a challenge to spinners, although it will not impede knitters who buy their yarn ready spun!

It is not all bad news though! As it is relatively coarse and straight, the wool has a generally low crimp, but the fleece is dense, strong, and springy, making yarns which are hard-wearing, crisp, and firm. For example, Hebridean fibers produce a more distinct texture in a fabric made from dark yarn than Black Welsh Mountain. They also make strong weaving yarns and are an excellent way to add natural color and contrast in rugs and blankets.

Hebridean wool is good too for strong outerwear, bags, cushions, and socks. The following patterns are for a handbag and a black-and-white cushion based on traditional Scottish Sanquahar designs. However, the yarn will cheerfully work as a crisper and harder wearing alternative to the patterns for Black Welsh Mountain, Castlemilk Moorit, Jacob, Manx Loagthan, and North Ronaldsay, as well as Ryeland or Zwartbles yarns.

YARN USER'S GUIDE

Good for ...
- Weaving
- Durable knitted items such as outerwear, and bags, and socks
- Blankets and rugs
- Felting

Not so good for ...
- Dyeing
- Lightweight items
- Wearing next to the skin

Dark and lustrous, yarn from from the fleece of the Hebridean sheep makes a durable fabric ideal for hard-wearing outer garments, rugs and bags.

Hebridean handbag

By Sue Blacker

This stylish and chunky bag is designed either to sit neatly under the arm, resting just above the hip, or as a satchel to carry letter paper-sized documents and files. There is also an option to knit it with a curved base for a modern, slouchy style.

You start by knitting the strap—which also acts as the base and sides of the bag—and then add panels for the front and back (which extends over the front to act as the flap). The strap is decorated with a simple cable stitch, which is a perfect introduction to cable knitting for the beginner, and will please more experienced knitters by being easy to knit as the work grows. Adjust the length of the strap to suit your style—measure an existing bag and work accordingly.

The bag is closed using a button and loop fastening. This can be replaced with a large press stud covered with a tassel. Or make a bag without a flap and close with a button and loop across the top opening.

Two strands of Aran yarn are used for a chunky finish, so you can use a single color or mix two shades for a tweedy effect. You could also try making the strap in a single color and the body of the bag in mixed colors or

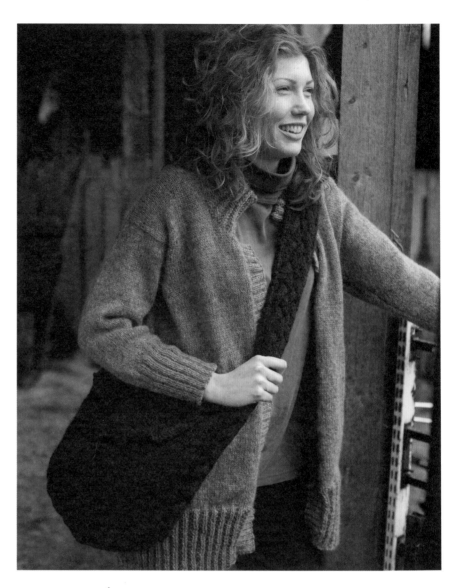

YARN REQUIREMENTS
Hebridean Aran wool
• Total amount of wool by weight and approximate length:
Handbag 350 g/532 yds (490 m)
Shoulder or slouch bag 650 g/988 yds (910 m)

a contrasting color. The two strands of chunky wool also make it quick to knit.

Advanced knitters can adapt the pattern, using a provisional cast-on for the strap and then binding off the two ends of the strap together once the bag has

been made up. A further adaptation would be to pick up and work the stitches for the front and back from the strap, joining the panels to the strap as they go. This will result in a very unstructured bag—stitched side seams will create a more rigid bag.

Method

THE STRAP

Using size 8 (5 mm) needles and two strands of wool, cast on 23 sts. Work in cable pattern as follows:

Row 1: S1, k1, p2, k15, p2, k2.
Row 2: S1, p1, k2, p15, k2, p1, k1.
Row 3: S1, k1, p2, k3, C6F, C6F, p2, k2.
Row 4: as row 2.
Row 5: as row 1.
Row 6: as row 2.
Row 7: S1, k1, p2, C6B, C6B, k3, p2, k2.
Row 8: as row 2.
Repeat rows 1-8 until work measures 42 in (107 cm) for handbag or 72 in (183 cm) for shoulder bag. Bind off.

Marking the position of the front and back on the strap
On a flat surface, spread out the strap, right side facing (cable pattern towards you). The seam joining the strap will be at one corner of the base of the bag.

MEASUREMENTS

Handbag: 10 in (25cm) wide and 6 in (15 cm) deep. Strap measures 18 in (46 cm)
Shoulder and slouch bag: 12 in (30 cm) high and 10 in (25 cm) wide. Strap measures 36 in (91.5 cm)

NEEDLES & NOTIONS

1 pair needles size 8 (5 mm)
Cable needle
Stitch markers (or safety pins)
1 crochet needle size 8 (5 mm)
1 pair double-pointed needles size 6 (4 mm)
Darning needle
1 large button.

GAUGE

Approx 13 sts x 17 rows = 4 in (10 cm) over stocking stitch using two strands of wool on size 8 (5 mm) needles
Gauge is not particularly important as this design is measured throughout and the pieces can be fitted together as made.

ABBREVIATIONS (see also page 140)

C6F: slip next 3 stitches onto cable needle, hold at front of work, k3 then k sts from cable needle.
C6B: slip next 3 stitches onto cable needle, hold at back of work, k3 then k sts from cable needle.

SKILL LEVEL

HANDBAG

Working from left to right, place a marker at 12 in (30 cm) (marker A), 6 in (15 cm) (marker B), 18 in (46 cm) (marker C). Adjust the measurement between markers B and C so there is 6 in (15 cm) left at the end.
The portion of strap between the end and A marks the base, A to B is one side panel, B to C is the strap, and C to the other end is the second side panel.

Handbag strap dimensions			
start a	b	c	
12 in	6 in	18 in	6 in
30cm	15cm	46cm	15cm
Base	Side	Strap	Side

SHOULDER BAG

Working from left to right, place a marker at 12 in (30 cm) (marker A), 12 in (30 cm) (marker B), 36 in (91.5 cm) (marker C). Adjust the measurement between markers B and C so there is 6 in (15 cm) left at the end.
The portion of strap between the end and A marks the base, A to B is one side panel, B to C is the strap, and C to the other end is the second side panel.

Shoulder bag strap dimensions			
start a	b	c	
12 in	12 in	36 in	12 in
30cm	30cm	91.5cm	30cm
Base	Side	Strap	Side

SLOUCH BAG

The base and sides are stitched to the rounded edge of the bag. Simply divide the strap in half so that the join is in the middle of the base when sewing up.

HAND- AND SHOULDER BAG FRONT (knit 1)

With cable pattern facing upwards, and using crochet hook and two strands of wool, pick up 42 sts from start to A. Insert the hook through the holes of the knit stitches to give a neat finish. Transfer the stitches onto a knitting needle.
Work in stocking stitch until knitting measures 6 in (15 cm) for handbag or 12 in (30 cm) for shoulder bag, ending with a purl row. Bind off.

HAND- AND SHOULDER BAG BACK AND FLAP (knit 1)

With cable pattern facing upwards, and using crochet hook and two strands of wool, pick up 42 sts from other side of the strap from start to A, in the same way as for the front. Work in stocking stitch until knitting measures 6 in (15 cm) for handbag or 12 in (30 cm) for shoulder bag. Place a marker at the end of this row. This forms the back and the extent to which you will need to sew the back to the sides of the bag. Continue knitting for a further 6 in (15 cm) ending with a purl row.

Shaping the flap

Next row: K3, s1, k1, psso. Knit to last 5 sts, s1, k1, psso, k3.
Next row: purl.
Repeat these two rows 6 times (30 sts remain). Bind off.
The flap will roll up of its own accord; sew this back into place at either end.

SLOUCH BAG FRONT
(make 1)

With 2 strands of yarn, cast on 8sts.
Row 1: purl
Row 2 (RS): knit to last stitch, cast on 8 sts
Row 3: purl to last stitch, cast on 8 sts
Row 4: knit
Row 5: purl
Row 6: as row 2
Row 7: as row 3
Row 8: knit
Row 9: purl
Row 10: (RS) knit to last stitch, cast on 4 sts
Row 11: purl to last stitch, cast on 4 sts
Repeat non increase and increase rows with 4 sts increase for next 4 rows, then with 3 sts increase for next 8 rows and 2 st increase for next 8 rows to make a total of 76 sts.

Now continue in stocking stitch until work measures 10 in (25 cm) from cast on edge. Bind off.

SLOUCH BAG BACK
(make 1)

Work as for front, but instead of binding off when work measures 10 in (25cm), place a marker at the end of this row. This forms the back and the extent to which you will need to sew the back to the sides of the bag. Continue work for a further 6 in (15 cm) ending with a purl row. Shape flap as for shoulder bag.

FINISHING OFF

Hand- and shoulder bag

With right sides facing, sew back and front to sides, using markers as a guide. Sew on a large button in the centre of the front approx 2.5 in (7 cm) from the base.

Slouch bag

Mark center of base on front and back. Join strap ends, then pin to front, matching the center of the base to the join in the strap. Repeat for the back. You can hide the seams inside the bag, or keep them on the outside as a feature, in which case use back stitch.

Crochet or knit an I-cord, or plait some wool to make a cord approx 2 in (5 cm) long with a tail of 4 in (10 cm) on each side and sew on to the base of the flap to provide a fastening for the button. Sew the loop together at the top

so that it will fasten around the button tightly.
Wash bag. Block to dry, or dry flat and steam press to correct shape when dry.
To stiffen the base more, cut two lengths of drinking straw or wood skewer and oversew into each corner across the width of the base.

Sanquhar cushion

By Tina Barrett

Sanquhar knitting designs developed in the town of that name in Dumfries and Galloway, Scotland. The traditional two-color designs date from the 1700s and were named after people, events, and everyday things including The Duke, Rose, Trellis, Drum, Coronet, Glendyne, Midge and Flea, Shepherd's Plaid and Prince of Wales, and Fleur de Lys. They were knitted in the round to create items such as gloves and stockings and sold to bring vital income to many families.

This cushion takes two traditional geometric Sanquhar stitch patterns and reinterprets them for flat knitting to make an attractive cushion in Hebridean and white wool (we have used white Jacob yarn).

The front is worked as a single piece and the back as two pieces, which meet in the middle, and may be finished with a zip or buttons or hooks and loops.

YARN REQUIREMENTS

• Total amount of wool by weight and approximate length

Yarn A: Pure Hebridean Wool DK 200 g/476 yds (440 m)
Yarn B: Pure Pale Jacob Wool DK 100 g/238 yds (220 m)

Method

FRONT (make one)

Using size 6 (4 mm) needles and Hebridean yarn (A), cast on 95 sts.

Work 2 rows in stocking stitch, then joining in Jacob yarn (B) work as follows:

Row 1: K10, work 24 sts of Row 1 of the Duke chart (right hand border), work 27 sts of Row 1 of the Midge and Fly chart, work 24 sts of Row 1 of the Duke chart (left hand border), k10.
Row 2: p10, work 24 sts of Row 2 of the Duke chart (left hand border), work 27 sts of Row 2 of the Midge and Fly chart, work

24 sts of Row 2 of the Duke chart (right hand border), p10. These 2 rows set the pattern for the cushion front.

Continue to work the chart repeats until you have completed the Duke borders 4 times. Then, continue as set until you have completed 12 further rows of the Duke border.

Work 2 rows in stocking stitch using Hebridean (A). Bind/cast off.

BACK (make two)

Using Hebridean (A) and size 6 (4 mm) needles, cast on 97 sts. Work as follows using the 2 colors stated in brackets:
Row 1: P2(A), *k3(B), p2(A)* repeat from * to * to end of row.
Row 2: K2(A), *p3(B), k2(A)* repeat from * to * to end of row.
Row 3: P2(A), * k1(B),k1(A),k1(B), p2(A)* repeat from * to * to end of row.
Row 4: As Row 2.
Repeat Rows 1-4 once more, then work Rows 1 and 2 once.

Change to Hebridean (A) and work in stocking stitch for a further 8.5 in (22 cm) ending with a purl row.
Bind/cast off.

FINISHING

Darn in loose yarn ends. Pin and block pieces into shape.

With right sides facing, place the two back flaps over the front piece, overlapping the ribbed bands and lining up all edges. Pin and then sew along all sides. Turn right side out, insert cushion pad through back flap. Or, sew along three sides. Attach zip, hooks or buttons and loops to fourth side. Turn right side out and insert cushion pad then close fastening.

MEASUREMENTS
Finished cushion size:
16 x 16 in (41 x 41 cm) square

SKILL LEVEL

NEEDLES & NOTIONS
A pair of size 6 (4 mm) needles
16 in (41 cm) cushion pad
Zip, buttons or hooks (optional)

GAUGE
25 sts x 26 rows = 4 in (10 cm) using size 6 (4 mm) needles over Duke and Midge and Fly stitch pattern.
22 sts x 30 rows = 4 in (10 cm) using size 6 (4 mm) needles over stocking stitch.

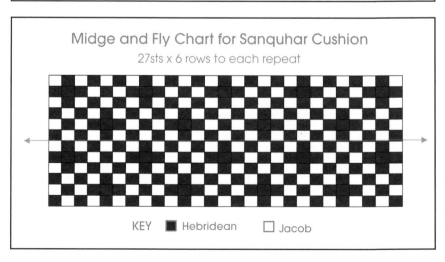

Sanquhar Cushion Charts for Duke Design Side Borders
Midge and Fly Chart will sit between the borders at point of red arrow.
Duke Design Charts 24 sts x 25 rows each

Left side border   Right side border

KEY   ■ Hebridean   □ Jacob

Midge and Fly Chart for Sanquhar Cushion
27sts x 6 rows to each repeat

KEY   ■ Hebridean   □ Jacob

Herdwick fleece

Perhaps because the eyes are set more to the front than on many sheep, or perhaps because the head is relatively rounded, the Herdwick has one of the most distinctive and attractive sheep faces. They are considered the hardiest of British breeds and are said to resort to eating their own fleeces if necessary when there is too much snow or too little grass.

Herdwick sheep have a heavy, dense fleece with a fine undercoat, coarser fibers and kemp and sometimes a stronger ruffle or mane at the neck and shoulders. This coat is adapted for the harsh weather of their traditional home, the high, exposed, and rain-swept Cumbrian fells of the Lake District. Farmers find the fleece dries out faster than that of other breeds after rain.

They are free to roam over long distances to find enough to eat and have a unique inherited knowledge of the fells, known as "heaf". This tells them which areas of the hills—much like an upland desert to a stranger—their flock has traditionally grazed and enables them to navigate their way home. No: sheep are not stupid!

Like many mountain sheep, the Herdwick spends time tupping and lambing in the valleys. The lambs and ewes return to the hills after lambing, and the ewes spend the winter on the hills. Ram lambs are fattened in the valley; ewe lambs are kept there to gain strength.

A famous Herdwick farmer was the children's author and illustrator Beatrix Potter, who farmed around Hawkshead. At her death in 1943, she left all her fifteen farms of 4,000 acres (16 square kilometres) of land to the National Trust to be grazed by Herdwick sheep.

Solidly built with sturdy legs, the Herdwick is not a large sheep and weighs in at 77–99 lbs (35–45 kg) for ewes and 143–165 lbs (65–75 kg) for rams.

BREED AT A GLANCE

Sheep type: Native breed.
Appearance: The rams generally have curling horns but the ewes have none. White heads and legs; born dark brown or black, gradually fading through gray to white as they get older.
Rare breeds status: Vulnerable.
Further information:
UK breed society: www.herdwick-sheep.com.
History: Recorded from the 12th century. They are thought variously to originate from Viking imports or the Spanish Armada. Unlike the other sheep inhabiting the high western pastures of the UK, they are not part of the northern short-tail family.

Aran yarn overdyed
purple

scoured
fleece

FLEECE FACT FILE
Fleece weight: 2–4 lbs (1.5–2 kg)
Staple length: 2–4 ins (10–20 cm)
Micron count: 35 and over
Crimp: Firm
Handle: Dense, with mixed fibers
Natural colors: Mostly gray,
sometimes brown or near-white
Mixed colors: Grays and browns,
Luster: Very straight

Close-up of knitted Aran sample

raw fleece

Aran yarn
overdyed olive

carded fleece

Aran yarn
overdyed plum

Herdwick yarn

Herdwick fleece is coarse and dense, and although there is some soft undercoat, most of it is quite harsh, thick, and stiff. Nevertheless, the color is one of the most attractive, being varied in whites, grays, and browns all through the fleece, so yarns and felt have a wonderful depth of natural tweedy colors.

The thick fleeces, with their relatively short staple length, can only be used for woollen spinning and are best used for thicker, Aran or chunky yarns. The lovely natural colors are ideal for rugs and carpets, and also for hard-wearing woven travel rugs. The fleece contains kempy fibers which do not take dye, but give the dyed yarns a lovely heathery result.

Writing with the experience of having knitted and worn a Herdwick pullover, I can certainly say it is possible, but most people will find the wool too scratchy. So we have chosen accessories to show off the color and texture of the yarn in the home, with tea and coffee cosies. However, Herdwick yarn will also work on bags, cushions, and hard-wearing body-warmers and waistcoats, so the patterns for the Hebridean bag, Jacob socks, and North Ronaldsay would also work. If blended with mohair, the wool will take dye even better and becomes softer.

YARN USER'S GUIDE

Good for ...
- Carpets
- Felting
- Outerwear
- Home accessories
- Woven rugs

Not so good for ...
- Wearing next to the skin
- Dyeing for solid colors

Dyed Herdwick yarn has an appealing heathery appearance thanks to the kemp in the fleece.

Herdwick tea, cafetière, and egg cosies

By Sue Blacker

This very easy design is made to measure for your cafetière or teapot. Each item can be finished with a pom-pom or tassels. The originals were designed using a combination of dyed and naturally colored yarn, but you can choose just Herdwick Hog (brown) and older Herdwick (gray and/or white) if you prefer, and use one, two or three colors, as available.

The design has only one pattern row, and instructions are given to make stripes, using three colors in turn, but you can use a single color or stripes of as many colors as you like! Striped items normally need joins between the colors, but we have used narrow stripes so that you can just carry the spare color up the side of the work to save breaking off and re-joining all the time.

To carry the yarn up the side of the work neatly, pass the yarn not being used between the first slipped stitch of the row from front to back at the beginning of each odd numbered row (i.e. where the strands are!). You will need to take a little

care not to get in a tangle, but it is not difficult! It makes life easier if you take yarn from the center of a ball, rather than from the outside.

To get started, you must measure the cafetière or teapot for which you are making the cosy and use this to calculate the stitches and rows required. You can

YARN REQUIREMENTS

Herdwick Aran yarn
• Total amount of wool by weight and approximate length for tea and cafetière cosies: 3 x 50g/76 yds (70 m) Use spare yarn for the egg cosies.
The yarn is used double throughout.

also use the dimensions of an existing cosy. Don't worry if your measurements are not exact—a little bit too big is

MEASUREMENTS
The cosies are made to measure

NEEDLES & NOTIONS
A pair of size 10 (6 mm) needles

GAUGE
Not required as items are made to measure.

ABBREVIATIONS
See Knitting Know-How (page 140)

SKILL LEVEL

Method

TEA COSY
Worked in two pieces, and then seamed up each side, leaving space for the handle and spout. The width of each side is half the circumference of the pot. Add 1.5 in (3 cm) for easing to both sides. For example, if the pot is 15.5 in (40 cm) around, your knitting will be 9 in (23 cm) wide (half of 15.5 in (40 cm) plus 1.5 in (3 cm)).

CAFETIÈRE COSY
Worked in one piece, and covers the whole cafetière (it is removed for pouring). The width of your knitting will be the circumference of the cafetière including the handle. Add 1.5 in (3 cm) for easing to both sides. For example, if the pot is 15.5 in (40 cm) around, the knitting will be 17 in (46 cm) wide 15.75 in plus 1.5 in (40 cm plus 6 cm).

TEA AND CAFETIÈRE COSIES
Measure the overall height of the teapot or cafetière, from the base to the center of the lid. This will be the length to knit. If you want, make it 4 in (10 cm) longer to turn over the rim.

PATTERN
Tweedy stripes: start in your first two colors (A and B, whichever you prefer), knit 2 rows, then drop A and add in the next color, C, knit 2 rows, then drop the B, to add in the A again and knit 2 rows, and so you have 6 rows, with the first 2 in A and B, the second 2 in B and C and the third 2 in C and A, then go back to A and B and repeat the process. Continue, changing color every two rows. The ends and balls of wool will always be at one side of the work.
Plain stripes: use 2 strands of A, followed by 2 strands of B, then 2 strands of C and work 2 rows in each color. (Or use two colors if prefered.)

SIDES (knit 1 or 2)
Using size 10 (6 mm) needles and two strands of yarn, cast on 10 sts loosely for every 2 in (5 cm) of the side measurement (e.g. if the circumference is 8 in (20 cm), cast on 40 sts; if 6 in (15 cm), it is 30 sts; if 10 in (25 cm), it is 50 sts, etc.). *This only works with multiples of 4 sts plus 1*, so add on extra sts to make this work (e.g. for 6 in (15 cm)), which would need 30 sts, make it 33, and for 40 and 50 stitches, make it 41 and 53, etc.)
Row 1: SL1, *k2, p2*, repeat from * to * to last 4 sts, k2, p1, k1. All following rows, as Row 1 using narrow striped pattern as described above.

Continue until work measures the correct length. Bind off.

EGG COSY
These are worked with a single strand of yarn. Make in one color and add pom-poms in a contrasting color. Or make stripes from spare yarn. Make a different color—or pattern—for each family member!

SIDES (knit 1)
Using size 10 (6 mm) needles and your chosen color, cast on 29 sts loosely.
Row 1: SL1, *k2, p2*, repeat from * to * to last 4 sts, k2, p1, k1.
All following rows, as Row 1 Continue with pattern and stripes until work measures 4 in (10 cm) long. Bind off.

MAKING UP
Break off yarn, leaving a long thread, and use a darning needle to thread through your stitches and pull up tightly to gather at the top and overstitch to secure. Using the same thread, sew down the side seam—leaving spaces for the teapot spout and handle—and sewing in any loose ends. Fasten securely. Sew a pom-pom or tassel securely over the center of the gathered top.(See page 141.)

Jacob fleece

There is only one truly and distinctly spotted sheep: the black-and-white Jacob. They have a characteristic white blaze on the face and a tendency to develop more dark patches at the front than at the back. Some Jacob sheep have a few large dark patches, while a very few are almost like Dalmatian dogs with many small spots.

Little is known about the origins of the Jacob sheep beyond the fact that they came to the UK from the Middle East, possibly via Spain. Spotted sheep can been seen in Egyptian wall paintings dated to 1800 BC.

British breeding has tended to select for larger sheep, to make them more commercial, but the U.S. breeders have focused more on the decorative characteristics, possibly closer to the breed's primitive roots, so the fleeces, sheep, and sizes vary. The fact that much less sheep meat is eaten in the U.S. may be a factor in this.

Despite their decorative appearance, Jacob sheep are hardy and a viable commercial breed. A decent size, the ewes weigh 132–143 lbs (60–65 kg) and the rams 176–220 lbs (80–100 kg).

While it is a minority breed, the sheep are not rare in the UK. However, having been a parkland sheep it was considered to be a hobby animal. When the Rare Breeds Survival Trust was established in 1974, it classified the Jacob as a Minority Breed as there were only 2,000 registered breeding ewes. Today, the Jacob is a success story with more than 5,000 registered ewes. In 1989 there were 400 animals registered in the U.S. By 2006, more than 10,000 Jacob sheep were known, but it is listed as a rare breed by the American Livestock Breeds Conservancy.

BREED AT A GLANCE

Sheep type: Primitive.

Appearance: 2–6 horns, piebald white/black fleece (UK standard is for two-thirds white and one-third black).

Rare breeds status: Threatened in the U.S. No longer considered at risk in the UK.

Further information: UK breed society: www.jacobsheep.org.uk.
US breed society: www.jsba.org.

History: Claimed to have originated in Mesopotamia in Biblical times, taking its name from Jacob in the Old Testament, who became rich from rearing a flock of spotted sheep. Like other colored sheep, used as parkland sheep and from the mid-eighteenth century were imported to the UK and the U.S. for this purpose.

scoured fleece

carded fleece

raw fleece

FLEECE FACT FILE
Fleece weight: 3–5 lbs (1.75–2.75 kg)
Staple length: 3–6 in (8–15 cm)
Micron count: 25–28, sometimes finer
Crimp: Medium, not distinct
Handle: Medium to firm
Natural colors: White, black
Mixed colors: Light gray, mid-gray, dark gray
Luster: Semi-luster (white); none (black)

Close-up of pure DK knitted sample

50/50 mid-gray
Jacob/mohair
worsted spun yarn

pure white DK
yarn

50/50 dark gray
Jacob/mohair
blend 4-ply
worsted spun yarn

pure very
dark DK yarn

Jacob yarn

Jacob fleece is of medium thickness, length, and softness, and it is incredibly versatile as a result. The only things it is not really suitable for are lace and baby clothes; it is also not as easy to felt as some other fibers.

Although most Jacob wool is "black and white", the dark color can be anything from mauve-brown or blue-brown to off-black, and the white wool is a creamy color. Separating the colors of wool into dark, light, and "in-between" gives three shades: cream, very dark brown, and brown-gray. These three can be re-mixed to create at least two further intermediate shades.

There may be significant differences of texture, thickness, and even staple length between the white and dark fleece on individual Jacob sheep, although this is considered a defect in fleece judging. For example, the dark wool tends to be coarser, possibly with more kemp and shorter than the pale wool, which also sometimes has quite noticeable luster. The lock formation may also be different, with the dark wool woollier and with an indistinct crimp, and the pale wavier and with straighter locks.

This range of wool from a single sheep is only matched by the varied colors achieved (but mainly individually) by Shetland sheep. In addition, all paler versions and blends of the color-sorted Jacob shades will dye happily.

The fleeces are excellent for hand-spinning, and work in both woollen- and worsted-spun yarns, and from 4-ply to chunky weights. However, the Jacob's fibers are too thick and bulky to make a lace-weight yarn.

The wool can be softened by blending with mohair, which not only makes it more hard-wearing but also enhances the luster and the dyeing results. We have also found that Jacob blends well with alpaca, which makes soft weaving yarns for scarves. Natural Jacob, as well as blends with mohair, make wonderful blankets, throws, and shawls.

Jacob is versatile and, apart from the Cotswold and some Gotland or fine Shetland patterns, may be used as an alternative for every pattern in this book! We have chosen a chunky jacket, knitted in two differently colored strands of double knitting yarn to show off the natural colors, and a pair of socks made in a 50/50 blend of Jacob with mohair for extra wear.

If the many natural shades of Jacob yarn are not enough, it dyes well. Here it is used to knit the cardigan on page 126.

YARN USER'S GUIDE

Good for ...
- Blending, weaving, dyeing
- Hand-spinning
- A wide range of weights of yarn
- Versatile knitting yarn
- Textured and cabled designs (if worsted-spun or Guernsey)

Not so good for ...
- Dyeing darker wool
- Lace-weight yarn
- Baby clothes
- Felting

Jacob cable jacket

By Myra Mortlock

This cosy jacket is quick to knit and makes a perfect introduction to knitting cables. It is worked using two strands of worsted-weight or DK yarn. This means you can choose two different shades to create a tweed effect (as shown in the photographs), or use just one color. The jacket is also quick to knit.

The body and sleeves have a chunky texture thanks to the garter and moss stitch panels, which frame a central double cable on the back, and cabled edges on the front. The jacket is designed to be closed with a large button— or you can use a brooch or shawl pin.

You can work the collar in moss stitch, which will lie flat, or reverse stocking stitch, which results in an attractive curled edge. Similarly, the center-front bands can be worked in moss stitch, rather than the garter stitch shown. This will result in flat, rather than curled, edges.

The drape of the jacket can be altered by knitting loosely or more tightly—knit a trial swatch and change needle size to create the effect you want (see notes on Gauge).

It is a large garment, and so it becomes quite heavy as is it knitted, but think how warm it will keep you!

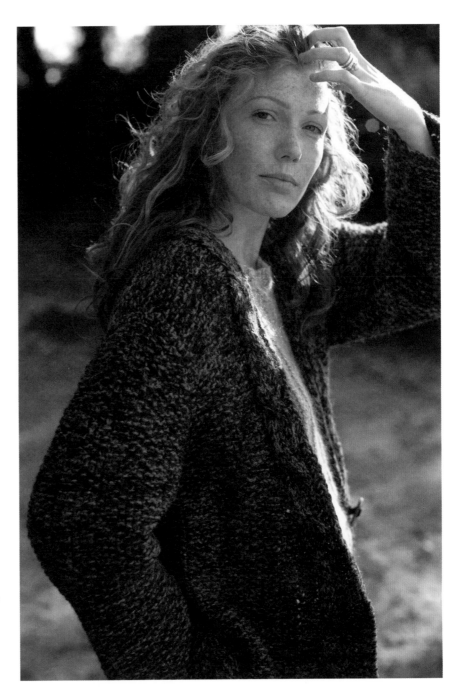

YARN REQUIREMENTS

Jacob worsted-weight/DK
• Total amount of wool by weight and approximate length:
Small 900 g/2,165 yds (1,980 m)
Medium 1,000 g/2,405 yds (2,200 m)
Large 1,100 g/2645 yds (2,420 m)
• Yarn used doubled throughout. Use a single color throughout, or equal amounts of two different colors for a tweedy effect.

Method

NOTE: working with two strands of yarn is easy, but occasionally you will only pick up one, so check each row. You will usually find the mistake on the next row. Use a crochet hook to pick up and link in the extra strand.

BACK (make 1)

With size 10½ (7 mm) needles and two strands of yarn, cast on 69 (75, 81) sts.
First row:
Size S: *k3, p1, k1, p1*, repeat * to * 3 times; set sts for center cable panel p2, k6, p2, k1, p2, k6, p2; *p1, k1, p1, k3*, repeat * to * 3 times.
Size M: k3, *p1, k1, p1, k3*, repeat * to * 3 times; set sts for center cable panel p2, k6, p2, k1, p2, k6, p2; *k3, p1, k1, p1*, repeat * to * 3 times, k3.
Size L: *k3, p1, k1, p1*, repeat * to * 4 times; set sts for center cable panel p2, k6, p2, k1, p2, k6, p2; *p1, k1, p1, k3* repeat * to * 4 times.
Repeat this row, working cable panel on the center panel sts. Continue until back measures 22 (23, 24) in (56 (58, 61) cm).

Underarm shaping (RS facing and maintaining pattern):
Rows 1 and 2: bind/cast off 3 (4, 5) sts, work to end.
Rows 3 and 4: bind/cast off 2 (3, 4) sts, work to end.
Rows 5 to 10: bind off 1 st, work to end. 53 (55, 57) sts remain.
Continue working in pattern until back measures 30 (31, 32) in (approx 76 (78, 81) cm).
RS facing, work 18 (19, 20) sts. Bind off center 17 sts. Work to end.
Working on one shoulder WS facing, work 1 row without shaping. RS facing, s1, k1, psso, work to end.
Repeat these 2 rows.
Work 1 row without shaping.

FINISHED SIZES

Garment bust measurement:
46 (50, 56) in (118 (126, 142) cm)
Length from back of the neck to the hem:
31 (32, 33) in (79 (81.5, 84) cm)
Instructions are given for the smallest size first, followed by medium and large in brackets

NEEDLES & NOTIONS

1 pair needles size 10½ (7 mm)
Cable needle
2 stitch holders or lengths of waste yarn
1 large button

GAUGE

Approx 12 sts x 16 rows = 4 in (10 cm) over stocking stitch on size 10½ (7 mm) needles
Adjust needle size to give required tension.

ABBREVIATIONS (see also page 140)

C6F: slip 3 sts onto the cable needle. Hold at front of work. K3, then k3 from cable needle.
C6B: slip 3 sts onto cable needle. Hold at back of work. K3, then k3 from cable needle.
Cable panel: Row 1: P2, k6, p2, k1, p2, k6, p2. Row 2: K2, p6, k2, p1, k2, p6, p2. Repeat except for Row 5 and every following 12 row when RS facing: P2, C6B, p2, k1, p2, C6F, p2.

Bind off 16 (17, 18) sts.
Complete other shoulder, reversing the shaping.

FRONTS (make 2)

Note: the front side seam edges are worked in moss st. The center front bands are worked in garter st. The shoulder seam lies about 1 in (2 cm) towards the back, and the cable panel is extended to wrap around and graft together at center back neck. To make a neat edge to the neckline, slip the first st on each row as follows: s1, p4, k6, p2tog, p1 and continue in pattern.

Start with right front, which has an integrated buttonhole band. With size 10½ (7 mm) needles and two strands of yarn, cast on 42 (45, 48) sts.
Row 1: Sizes S and L: k5, p2, k6, p2, *p1, k1, p1, k3* Repeat to last 3 sts p1, k1, p1.
Size M: k5, p2, k6, p2, *k3, p1, k1, p1* Repeat to end.
Work rows 2–4 in pattern as set.
Row 5: RS facing, k5, p2, C6F, p2, work in pattern to end.
Repeat C6F every 12th row. Continue until work measures 15 in (38 cm).
Work buttonhole as follows:
RS facing, k3, turn and working on these 3 sts, k4 rows. Break yarn, leaving about 4 in (10 cm) tail of yarn.
Rejoin yarn to main knitting, and, continuing to work cable pattern every 12 rows, work 5 rows. WS facing, work across all sts. Work a further 4 rows.

Shape V-neck by decreasing at front edge and between the cable panel and the main pattern as follows:
RS facing, s1, k1, psso, k3, p2, k6, p2 together, p1, continue in

pattern to end. Work all WS rows in pattern and without shaping.
Next RS row: s1, k1, psso, k2, p2, k6, p2tog, p1, work to end of row in pattern.
Following RS row: at this point the garter st buttonhole band changes to reverse st st to create a roll-over edge for the neck line.
Continue decreasing on alternate rows until 34 (35, 36) sts remain.
Work without shaping until piece measures same as the back to underarm shaping.

Shape armhole
WS facing bind off 3 sts. Work in pattern to end.
Work 1 row.
Next WS row bind off 2 sts.
Work 1 row.
Next 3 WS rows: bind off 1 st at start of row. 27 (28, 29) sts remain.

Shape shoulder and back neck.
Continue working in pattern until front measures the same as the back to shoulder shaping, then work a further 3 or 4 rows so that you end at armhole edge. Bind off 15 (16, 17) sts.
Continue on remaining 12 sts in cable and rollover

edge for a further 3 in (7.5 cm). Cut wool, leaving about 15 in (38 cm) and place sts on a length of spare wool or a stitch holder.

The left front is worked in the same way as the right front, reversing pattern and shaping, so that the cable edge and V-neck are in the center, and omitting the buttonhole. This means that the first row will start with cable and moss stitch panels and end p2, k6, p2, k5.

SLEEVES (make 2)

With size 10½ (7 mm) needles and two strands of yarn, cast on 45 (48, 51) sts.
All sizes: work 5 rows garter st for cuff.
Change to garter and moss st panels as set for the back.
Continue until sleeve measures 9 (8, 7) in (23, 20, 18) cm).
Increase 1 st at both ends of the next row.
Repeat increase row every 1.5 in (4 cm) until there are 55 (60, 63) sts.
Work on these sts until sleeve measures 16 (16.5, 17) in

(40.5 (42, 43) cm). If you would like the cuff to end at the knuckle, rather than the wrist, work a further 1 in (2.5 cm).
Shape to match armhole shaping by decreasing at the start of rows as follows:
Rows 1 and 2: bind off 4 sts.
Rows 3 and 4: bind off 3 sts.
Rows 5 and 6: bind off 2 sts.
Rows 7 and 8 bind off 1 st.
Work 2 rows. Then repeat rows 7 and 8. Repeat * to * twice.
Bind off 3 sts at the beginning of the next 2 rows, then 5 sts at the start of the following 2 rows.
Bind off all remaining sts.

MAKING UP

Join shoulder seams. Attach sleeves to armhole edges. Sew side and sleeve seams.
Adjust length of cable bands if needed so that they meet at center back neck. Place cable band sts back on needles, both pointing the same way. Using cable needle, join pieces by knitting together a st from each needle and casting off in the usual way. Join cable band to back so that join lies above center back.

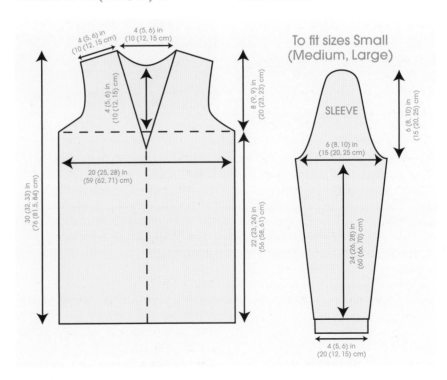

4 (5, 6) in (10 (12, 15) cm)

4 (5, 6) in (10 (12, 15) cm)

4 (5, 6) in (10 (12, 15) cm)

8 (9, 9) in (20 (23, 23) cm)

20 (25, 28) in (59 (62, 71) cm)

30 (32, 33) in (76 (81.5, 84) cm)

22 (23, 24) in (56 (58, 61) cm)

To fit sizes Small (Medium, Large)

SLEEVE

6 (8, 10) in (15 (20, 25) cm)

6 (8, 10) in (15 (20, 25) cm)

24 (26, 28) in (60 (66, 70) cm)

4 (5, 6) in (20 (12, 15) cm)

Socks for walking and rain boots

By Sue Blacker

This versatile pattern makes a great introduction to sock knitting. The socks are knitted from the top down and—apart from getting used to knitting on three needles rather than two—the pattern instructions are very simple to follow.

If you have never knitted a sock before, the heel instructions may not make a great deal of sense, but stick with them—if you do as indicated, the heel will turn.

There is no need to use a special sock yarn: any 4-ply yarn can be used for the walking boot socks, and choose an Aran yarn for the rain boot version.

Make them in any solid Jacob color, or try stripes all over the sock or just on the turnover of the rain boot design. If you're planning to make several pairs, make each one a little different to prevent friends and family stealing each others' socks—and (if you are lucky) it will help you to pair them up every time you wash them!

Use a pure Jacob yarn, or a blend with mohair, which will be harder wearing and feel softer when worn (this is not a contradiction—the mohair is both smooth, so it feels softer, and hard-wearing).

YARN REQUIREMENTS

• Total amount of wool by weight and approximate length:

Walking Boot socks
Jacob/mohair or Jacob 4-ply
150 g/570 yds (525 m)

Rain Boot socks
Jacob/mohair or Jacob Aran
200 g/262 yds (240 m)

FINISHED SIZES

The instructions and quantities given are for a medium adult sock around 9 in (23 cm) long in the foot, which is about US 7-9 in shoe sizes, but the socks can be made to measure. The leg section of the walking boot socks is 8 in (20 cm), and 13 in (33 cm) for the rain boot version, which has only a small cuff turnover, but you can lengthen or shorten this to suit.

To adjust the foot, measure the length of the foot, subtract 4 in (10 cm) for the heel and toe parts, and the measurement you are left with gives you the middle length to knit. The rain boot socks fit snugly on a 15 in (38 cm) calf. If you need something larger, cast on additional stitches (refer to the gauge to calculate the number needed) and then steadily reduce (over more rows than indicated) once you have completed the welt/turnover. Remember you will need more yarn if you do this.

NEEDLES & NOTIONS
Walking Boot socks
1 set of four size 2 (2.75 mm) double pointed needles
1 set of four size 3 (3.25 mm) double pointed needles
Rain Boot socks
1 set of four size 6 (4 mm) double pointed needles
1 set of four size 3 (3.25 mm) double pointed needles

GAUGE
Walking socks: 28 sts x 36 rows = 4 in (10 cm) square over main rib pattern
Rain Boot socks: 10 sts x 13 rows = 4 in (10 cm) square over stocking stitch
Adjust needle size to give required tension.

ABBREVIATIONS (see also page 140)
Stocking stitch: Normally one row k, one row p, but because you are knitting on three needles in turn, all sts will be k.
Graft off: Bind off the stitches together; use the third needle to help you.

Method
WALKING BOOT SOCKS (make 2)
Cast on 90 sts loosely using size 3 (3.25 mm) needles, with 30 sts on each of 3 needles and using Continental or long-tail cast-on. Change to size 2 (2.75 mm) needles and work 4 in (10 cm) in k1, p1, rib, (or k2, p1 if preferred). Change to size 3 (3.25 mm) needles and start rib pattern for leg: *k3, p2* and repeat from * to * until pattern section measures 8 in (20 cm). Next round: knit, decreasing evenly to 56 sts (19 on each of 2 needles and 18 on the third). Then work 9 rounds in stocking stitch (i.e. knit all stitches).

Divide for heel: k14, slip last 14 sts of round (from third needle) onto other end of the working needle, making 28 sts for heel and placing remaining 28 sts on two needles for instep.

Heel flap (knitted back and forth)
Row 1: sl 1 purlwise, purl to end.
Row 2: sl 1 purlwise with yarn behind, knit to end. Repeat until 17 rows have been worked.

Heel turn (knitted back and forth)
Row 1: k19, sl 1, k1, psso, turn.
Row 2: sl 1, p10, p2 tog, turn.
Row 3: sl 1, k10, sl 1, k1, psso, turn. Repeat Rows 2 and 3 five times, then row 2 once more.
Next row: sl 1, k to end, 14 sts remain.

Instep
Pick up and knit 13 sts along the right side, then knit the 28 sts left on the 2 needles for the instep, then knit 13 sts up left side to make 68 sts including the 14 from heel flap and continue in the round on 3 needles. Slip the last 7 sts from the last round on to the left hand needle. Then arrange stitches so there are 21 sts each on needles 1 and 3, 26 sts on needle 2.
Continue in stocking stitch:
Round 1: k19, k2tog, k26, sl 1, k1, psso, k19.
Round 2 and 3: knit.
Round 4: k18, k2tog, k26, sl 1, k1, psso, k18.
Repeat rows 1-4 3 times (56 sts), to make 15 sts on needles 1 and 3, and 26 sts on needle 2. Continue until desired foot length is reached, but remember the toe will make it about 2 in (5 cm) longer.

Shape toe
Round 1: k11, k2tog, k2, sl 1, k1, psso, k22, k2tog, k2, sl 1, k1, psso, k11.
Round 2 and every alternate round: knit.
Round 3: k10, k2tog, sl 1, k1, psso, k20, k2tog, k2, sl1, k1, psso, k10. Repeat these rounds, until 24 sts remain. Divide sts so you have 12 each on 2 needles and graft off, or finish using Kitchener stitch (see page 141).

RAIN BOOT SOCKS
(make 2)

Cast on 52 sts quite loosely, using size 6 (4 mm) needles, with 17 on the first 2 needles and 18 on the third, using Continental or long-tail cast-on. Change to size 3 (3.25 mm) needles.

Welt: work 4 in (10 cm) in rounds in k1, p1, rib, (or k3, p1 rib, as preferred – to use k2, p1 rib you need to reduce by 1 st and only cast on 51 sts), decreasing 1 st in last round to leave 51 sts. If you want a full turnover, make this section 8 in (20 cm) long.

Leg: next round: change to 4 mm needles, decrease by k2tog at beginning of round and k2togtbl at end of round. Then work 4 rounds in stocking stitch (i.e. knit all stitches). Repeat these 5 rounds twice (or more if you cast on more stitches), making 45 sts, then continue in stocking stitch to 13 in (33 cm) or the leg length required.

Divide for heel k11, slip last 12 sts of round onto same needle, making 23 sts for heel and placing remaining 22 sts on two needles for instep.

Heel flap (knitted back and forth)
Row 1: sl 1, purl to end.
Row 2: sl 1, knit to end.
Repeat until 9 more rows have been knitted, then make row 1 again (total 12 rows).

Heel turn (knitted back and forth)
Row 1: k13, sl 1, k1, psso, turn.
Row 2: p4, p2tog, turn.
Row 3: k5, sl 1, k1, psso, turn.
Row 4: p6, p2tog, turn.
Continue until all sts are on one needle.
Next row: k7, leave sts on left needle.

Instep

Slip instep sts onto one needle to give you a spare needle. Using the spare needle, k6, pick up and knit 12 sts from side of heel, then using a second needle knit across 22 instep sts, then using the third needle pick up and knit 11 sts along other side, k7, to make 58 sts.

Continue in stocking stitch:
Round 1: knit.
Round 2: first needle: knit to last 3 sts, k2tog, k1, second needle: knit, third needle: k1, k2tog tbl, knit to end.
Repeat rounds 1–2 until 44 sts remain (14 rounds in total). Then continue until desired foot length is reached: but remember this is the foot, with heel in place so allow for the toe which will make it about 2 in (5 cm) longer.

Shape toe
Row 1: first needle: k to last 3 sts, k2tog, k1, second needle: k1, k2tog tbl, k to last 3 sts, k2tog, k1, third needle: k1, k2tog tbl, k to end.
Row 2: knit.
Repeat these rows 4 times until 24 sts remain.
Split the 24 sts into 12 on each of 2 needles and graft off, or finish using Kitchener stitch (see page 141).

Manx Loaghtan fleece

The first thing that you notice about Manx Loaghtan sheep is their impressive sets of horns. Some rams and ewes have four horns, while others have six, two, or, in the case of some ewes, none at all. Being active, the sheep can bend or break their horns, so a beautiful symmetrical set is somewhat rare. They are known to have grazed the hills of the Isle of Man since the eleventh century.

The Manx Loaghtan are small brown sheep, although they bleach to cream in the sun. The lambs are born black and gradually achieve their particular shade of brown during the first year. (It is possible to keep Manx Loaghtan sheep from bleaching by keeping them indoors and letting them graze by moonlight.)

However, as with most primitive sheep, there is a wide variety of shades of brown, usually getting paler, with more kemp fibers, with age. It is possible that differences in soil on the island cause fleeces to be darker brown in the north than in the south, although there may be a genetic reason for this.

They have long hairless legs and are lean, though selective breeding for meat has meant some are now larger and more solidly built. Normally ewes weigh around 77 lbs (35 kg) and rams 99 lbs (45 kg).

Living on a small island has inevitably tended to make these sheep rare, and they are classified as At Risk by the Rare Breeds Survival Trust, with fewer than 1,500 registered breeding ewes.

Manx Loaghtan meat from the Isle of Man gained Protected Designation of Origin from the European Community in 2009.

The breed is believed to be the closest relative of the extinct Jersey sheep. A flock now grazes there and supplies fleeces for a 5-ply Guernsey yarn used for the traditional local pullovers.

BREED AT A GLANCE

Sheep type: Primitive.

Appearance: Small, brown sheep with two, four, or six horns.

Rare breeds status: Classified "At Risk" by the UK Rare Breeds Survival Trust. A conservation breed in the U.S.

Further information: UK breed society: www.manxLoaghtansheep.org.

History: Originally from the Isle of Man, off the west coast of the UK. Their name in Manx, *lugh dhoan*, means mouse-brown. Although considered native to the Isle of Man, they are part of the northern short-tail family of primitive sheep also found in Scotland and Wales.

DK yarn

FLEECE FACT FILE
Fleece weight: 3–5 lbs (1.5–2 kg)
Staple length: 2.5–4 in (7–10 cm). A shearling might produce longer wool, perhaps up to 4.75 in (12 cm)
Micron count: Around 30
Crimp: Indistinct
Handle: Soft/medium
Natural colors: Nut-brown; may bleach to cream in the sun
Mixed colors: None
Luster: None

raw fleece

carded pure
Manx fleece

Aran yarn

Close-up of pure DK knitted sample.

4-ply yarn

carded
Hebridean/Manx
blend yarn

Manx Loaghtan yarn

Manx Loaghtan yarn is known for its unusual brown "moorit" color—some fleeces are fine and fluffy, but others are distinctly hairy and coarser. It knits into a lightweight but warm fabric, and is also good for weaving into heavier items.

The raw wool is quite short, with no luster and an indistinct crimp but good resilience and bulk. The best examples will happily make 4-ply yarns, but the majority of fleeces are more suitable for Double Knitting, Aran, or Chunky yarns.

The bulkiness makes for light, warm garments. With these properties in mind, we have chosen a scarf, hat, and mittens pattern, but the yarn will work well for the Black Welsh Mountain, Castlemilk Moorit, Hebridean, Herdwick, Jacob, North Ronaldsay, and Zwartbles designs.

The wool is hard-wearing and works well for woven tweeds, tartans, rugs, and blankets. It adds a contrast with naturally colored stripes and checks in white fabrics.

However, Manx Loaghtan fleece can be bitty and gives low yields when spun commercially. It is easier to

YARN USER'S GUIDE
Good for ...
- Hard-wearing, lightweight garments
- Sweaters and socks
- Blankets and rugs
- Blending
- Dyeing when blended
- Bulk, loft

Not so good for ...
- Garments worn next to the skin
- Baby clothes
- Drape

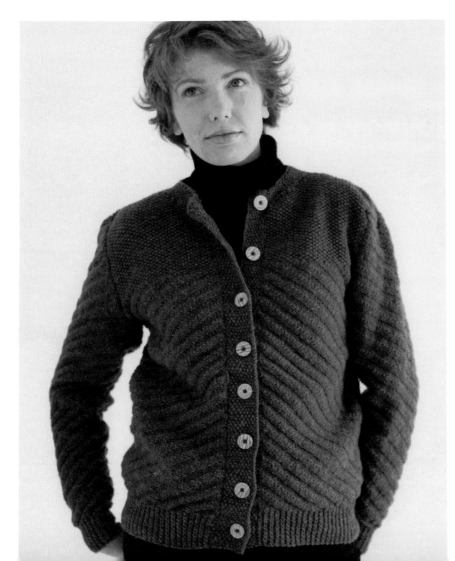

spin than Castlemilk Moorit, and they can be blended to improve the yield on Castlemilk. It unsuitable for worsted spinning.

Manx Loaghtan blends well with Hebridean to make a rich brown yarn with greater depth of color than the mid-brown alone, which can be dull if bleached fiber is included. It also works well with mohair to make a softer yarn in a pale coffee shade, which will dye to strawberry or golden hues. With mohair, it is possible to make a semi-worsted yarn.

Manx Loaghtan is ideal for sweaters and jackets. The results are hard-wearing, lightweight, and firrm to the touch.

Zig-zag scarf, hat, and mittens

By Sue Blacker

The zig-zag texture for this hat and scarf set is easy to follow as it is a combination of knit and purl stitches. They are fully reversible. For the set, with its stocking stitch mittens, I have chosen rich brown Manx Loagthan as it's such a lovely warming color, and the Double Knitting yarn gives density and warmth. They could be made for all the family in a range of rare breeds (can you suit the breed to the person?).

To keep the scarf and mittens together, add buttons to the ends of the scarf and buttonholes or loops to the mittens so they can be buttoned together.

The mittens are knitted in the round, but two needles can be used (instructions are given for this in brackets where appropriate).

Method

Twisted rib panel
For mittens over 7 sts
Row 1: p1, k2, p1, k2, p1.
Rows 2, 3, 4, 5 and 6: as row 1 if knitting in the round (but if using two needles, rows 2, 4 and 6, k1 p2 k1 p2 k1).
Row 7: p1, Tw2, p1, Tw2, p1.
Row 8: as row 1 (as row 2).

Shallow Zig-zag pattern
For Beanie Hat over 12 rows, multiples of 6sts.
The chart on page 94 shows the design over 39 sts. RS rows are worked from right to left, and WS from left to right. The last 4 rows reverse some from the first 8. Written instructions are below.

Deep Zig-zag design
For scarf over 48 rows, multiple of 6 sts plus 3.
The chart on page 94 shows the design and moss stitch edges. The second 24 rows reverse the first 24. Written instructions are also provided below.

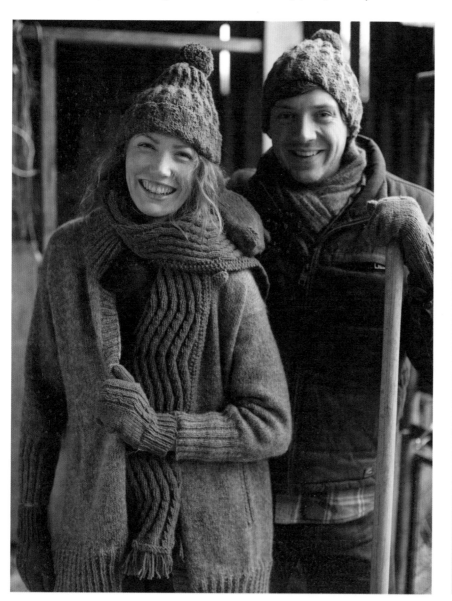

YARN REQUIREMENTS

Manx Loagthan Double Knitting yarn
• Total amount of wool by weight and approximate length:
Adult scarf:
250 g/595 yd (550 m)
Child's scarf:
200 g/476 yd (440 m)
Beanie hat:
100 g/238 yd (220 m)
Adult Mittens (all sizes):
100 g/238 yd (220 m)
Child's mittens (both sizes):
50 g/119 yd (110 m)

SCARF

Using size 7 (4.5 mm) needles, cast on 47 stitches for adult's scarf or 35 sts for child's scarf.

Base edge: rows 1 and 2: garter st (knit all sts)

Now start the Deep Zig-zag Design, with 3st moss st border at each side, slipping the first st and knitting the last st of every row to make an even edge:
Row 1: sl1, p1, k1, p1, (p3, k3) to last 7 sts, k3, p1, k1, p1, k1.
Row 2: sl1, k1, p1, k1, (p3, k3) to last 7 sts, p3, k1, p1, k2.
Row 3: as row 1.
Row 4: as row 2.
Row 5: sl1, p1, k1, p2, (k3, p3) to last 6 sts, k2, p1, k1, p1, k1.
Row 6: sl1, k1, p1, k1, p2, (k3, p3) to last 5 sts, k2, p1, k2.
Row 7: as row 5.
Row 8: as row 6.
Row 9: sl1, p1, k1, p2 (k3, p3) to last 5 sts, k2, p1, k2.
Row 10, sl1, k1, p1, k1 (k3, p3) to last 6 sts, k3, p1, k2.
Row 11: as row 9.
Row 12: as row 10.
Row 13: sl1, p1, k1, p4 (k3, p3) to last 4 sts, p1, k1, p1, k1.
Row 14: sl1, k1, p1, k4 (p3, p3) to last 4 sts, k1, p1, k2.
Row 15: as row 13.
Row 16: as row 14.
Row 17: sl1, p1, k1, p1, (p3, k3) to last 7 sts, p3, k1, p1, k1.
Row 18: sl1, k1, p1, k3 (p3, k3) to last 5 sts, p1, k1, p1, k2.
Row 19: as row 17.
Row 20: as row 18.
Row 21: sl1, p1, k1, p1, k2 (p3, k3) to last 5 sts, p2, k1, p1, k1.
Row 22: sl1, k1, p1, k2 (p3, k3) to last 6 sts, p2, k1, p1, k2.
Row 23: as row 21.
Row 24: as row 22.
Row 25: as row 1.
Row 26: as row 2.
Row 27: as row 1.
Row 28: as row 2.
Row 29: as row 21.
Row 30: as row 22.
Row 31: as row 21.
Row 32: as row 22.

Row 33: as row 17.
Row 34: as row 18.
Row 35: as row 17.
Row 36: as row 18.
Row 37: as row 13.
Row 38: as row 14.
Row 39: as row 13.
Row 40: as row 14.
Row 41: as row 9.
Row 42: as row 10.
Row 43: as row 9.
Row 44: as row 10.
Row 45: as row 5.
Row 46: as row 6.
Row 47: as row 5.
Row 48: as row 6.

Work in pattern until required length, finishing with 2 rows of garter stitch. There is no need to complete a set of 48 rows. However with complete repeats scarf design will be the same at each end. Bind off.

MEASUREMENTS

Adult scarf: 72 in (183 cm) long, 10 in (25.5 cm) wide
Child's scarf: 51 in (130 cm) long, 7 in (18 cm) wide
Beanie hat: made to measure, see below
Adult mittens (around hand): 6.75 (7.5, 8.25) in (17 (19, 21) cm)
Child's mittens (around hand): 5.5 (6) in (13.5 (15.5) cm)
Instructions are given for smallest size first, followed by medium and large in brackets. If only one is given, it applies to all sizes.

| SKILL LEVEL | ● |

NEEDLES & NOTIONS

Scarf: one pair size 7 (4.5 mm) knitting needles
Beanie: one pair size 6 (4 mm) knitting needles (or size 7 (4.5 mm) circular needle if preferred)
Mittens: one set of 4 DPN size 3 (3.25 mm) knitting needles, at least 8 in (20 cm) long and one set of 4 DPN size 3 (3.25 mm) knitting needles 5 in (12.5 cm) long (If knitting on two needles)
1 pair of size 3 (3.25 mm) needles)
2 buttons (wood or horn work well with Manx)
Stitch holders
Stitch marker (if knitting in the round)
Crochet hook

GAUGE

Approx 19 sts x 24 rows = 4 in (10 cm) over stocking stitch on size 7 (4.5 mm) needles
Adjust needle size to give required tension.

ABBREVIATIONS

See Knitting Know-How (page 140)

Tassel fringe

Wind yarn around a piece of card 3 in (8cm) wide and cut along one edge to make short threads. Using a crochet hook, and with each thread folded in half, insert hook into sts along end of scarf, pull through looped part of thread and pull ends through loop. You will need around half as many threads as stitches, depending on desired density of the fringe.

CHILDREN'S MITTENS

Using size 3 (3.25 mm) needles, cast on 36 (40) sts and work 18 rows of k1, p1 rib, then 2 rows of stocking stitch.
If you wish to button the mittens to the scarf, use two needles and leave a gap in the seam to act as the buttonhole.

Right mitten

Set up row: k6 (7) p1, k2, p1, k2, p1, k to end. Next row k (p) maintaining rib (see page 90).

Thumb

Row 1: k17 (19) m1, k2, m1, k17 (19). Work 3 rows stocking stitch after each increase row.
Row 5: k17 (19) m1, k4, m1, k17 (19).
Row 9: k17 (19) m1, k6, m1, k17 (19).
Row 13: k17 (19) m1, k8 m1, k17 (19).
Work 1 (3) rows stocking stitch.

Next row: k27 (29) turn, cast on 1 (2) sts and leave remaining sts on needle (st holder). Change to 5 in (12.5 cm) DPN.
Next row: p11 (12) turn, cast on 1 (2) sts, leave remaining sts on needles (st holder) work 1.5 (1.75) in (3.75 (4.5) cm) on 12 (14) sts (end with p row).

Shape thumb

Row 1: * k1, k2tog, rep from * to end (to last 2 sts k2).
Row 2: k (p).
Row 3: k2tog to end.
Break yarn, thread through sts and fasten off (sew seam).

Hand

Right side facing rejoin yarn, pick up and k 2 (4) sts from base of thumb then k to end of round (row). 36 (42) sts. Continue in st st and rib until hand measures 2.5 (3) in (6.5 (7.5) cm) from base of thumb.

Shape top

Row 1: k1, k2tog tbl, pattern 12 (15) k2tog, k2, k2tog tbl, pattern 12 (15) k2tog, k1.
Row 2: knit (purl) and all alt rounds (rows).
Row 3: k1, k2tog tbl, pattern 10 (13) k2tog, k2, k2tog tbl, pattern 10 (13) k2tog, k1.
Continue to dec in this way until 20 (26) sts are left.
Work one more row.
Turn mitten inside out, divide sts in half and place on two needles. Graft together or work a three-needle bind off (bind off and sew side seam).

Left mitten

Work as for right mitten except for pattern set up row: k23 (26) p1, k2, p1, k2, p1, k6 (7).
Next row knit (purl).

ADULT MITTENS

There are three sizes and may be worked entirely in stocking stitch or with twisted rib panels on the back of the hand. Work in the round or on two needles (instructions are given in square brackets where different).

Right mitten

Cast on 40 (44, 48) sts on size 3 (3.25 mm) DPN needles divided as follows 15 – 10 – 15 (16 – 12 – 16, 16 – 16 – 16) (or use two needles) and work in k2, p2, rib for 26 rows.
Large size only: work 2 rows st st.
Pattern set up row: large size only k10, p1, k2, p1, k2, p1, k to end. Next row knit (purl).
Set up row for small and medium sizes and start of thumb shaping for all sizes:

Shallow zig-zag pattern for hat (12 rows, multiples of 6 plus 3 sts)

Shallow zig-zag pattern for scarf (48 rows, multiples of 6 plus 3 sts)

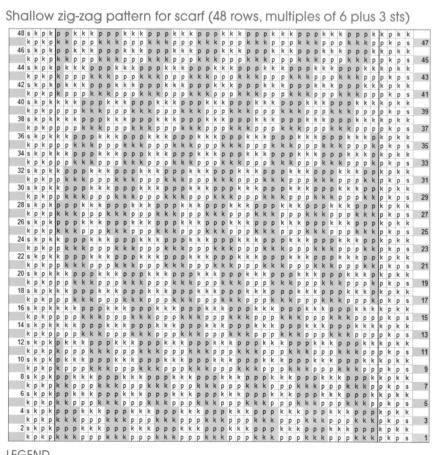

LEGEND

☐ k on RS; p on WS   ☐ p on RS; k on WS

Row 1: k8 (8, 10) p1, k2, p1, k2, p1, k4, (6, 6) m1, k2, m1, k19 (21, 23).
Continue Twisted Rib pattern and work 3 rows st st after this and following increase rows.

Shape for thumb
Row 1: k19 (21, 23) m1, k2, m1, k19 (21, 23). Work 3 rows in st st after this row and each of the following increase rows.
Row 5: k19 (21, 23) m1, k4, m1, k19 (21, 23).
Row 9: K19 (21, 23) m1, k6, m1, k19 (21, 23).
Row 13: k19 (21, 23) m1, k8 m1, k19 (21, 23).
Row 17: k19 (21, 23) m1, k10, m1, k19 (21, 23).

Small and medium sizes only work one row. .
Large Size only:
Row 21: k23, m1, k12, m1, k23.
Row 22: knit (purl). This completes thumb shaping.

Thumb
Row 1: k31 (33, 37) turn cast on 1 (2, 2) sts.
Row 2: p13, (14, 16) turn cast on 1 (2, 2).
Using hort DPNs divide these 14 (16, 18) sts between 3 needles: 5 - 4 - 5 (5 - 6 - 5, 6 - 6 - 6) and work in st st for 2 (2.25, 2.5)in (5.5 (6, 6.5) cm).
Shape top of thumb
Row 1: * k1, k2tog, rep from * to last 2 sts k2 (to the last st k1: to end).
Row 2: knit 1 round (purl 1 row).
Row 3: k2tog 5 times (k2tog 5 times k1, k2tog 6 times) Break yarn leaving a tail, thread through the remaining sts and fasten off (sew thumb seam).

Hand
Right side facing, rejoin yarn to sts on right hand needle. Pick up and k 6 (4, 6) sts along base of thumb, then k sts on left hand needle. 44 (46, 52) sts.
Work 1.75 (1.75, 2) in (4.5 (4.5 5) cm) in st st (end with purl row).

Continue, keeping pattern as set and working thumb, until hand measures 4 (4.25, 4.75) in (10 (11, 12) cm) from base of thumb.

Shape top
Row 1: k1, k2tog tbl, pattern 16 (17, 20) k2tog, k2, k2tog tbl, pattern 16 (17, 20) k2tog, k1.
Row 2 and all alt rows: knit (purl) keeping pattern correct.
Row 3: k1, k2tog tbl, pat 14 (15, 18) k2tog, k2, k2tog tbl, pat 14 (15, 18) k2tog, k1.
Continue to decrease in this way until 28 (30, 36) sts are left. Work one more row.
Divide these sts in half and place on two needles then graft together or work a three needle bind off (bind off and sew up seam).

Left mitten
Work as for right mitten except for pattern set up row:
Large Size only: K31, p1, k2, p1, k2, p1, k10.
Next row knit (purl).
Small and medium sizes and the start of thumb shaping for all sizes:
Row 1: k19 (21: 23), m1, k2, m1, k4 (6, 6), p1, k2, p1, k2, p1, k8 (8, 10).
Continue as right mitten.

BEANIE HAT
Making to measure
Measure the circumference of the head, including the ears, for which you are making the hat, or copy the size of an existing one. Add 2 in (5 cm) to your measurement to give the total width. For example, if the head is 23.5 in (60 cm) your knitting will be 25.5 in (65 cm) wide. For the length, measure from the ear lobes to the middle of the head. For the length to knit, add 3 in (8 cm) to allow for a turn over at the brim. (For a child's size, add 2 in (5 cm).) Omit turnover if you prefer.

Pattern
Using size 6 (4 mm) needles, cast on 10 sts loosely for every 2 in (5 cm) of calculated width (e.g. if the width is 24 in (60 cm), cast on 120 sts). This pattern requires an even number of sts, and multiples of 3 sts, so add extra to make this work (e.g. for 21.5 in (55 cm), which needs 110 sts, make it 114, etc.).

Work Shallow Zig-zag pattern as on chart opposite or as below.
Row 1: (k3, p3) to end.
Row 2: as round/row 1.
Row 3: p1 (k3, p3) to last 2 sts, p2.
Row 4: as round/row 3.
Row 5: p2, (k3, p3) to last st, p1.
Row 6: as round/row 5.
Row 7: (p3, k3) to end.
Row 8: as round/row 7.
Row 9: as row 5.
Row 10: as row 5.
Row 11: as row 3.
Row 12: as row 3.
Continue in pattern until work measures the required length, less 3 in (8 cm) for crown.

Shape crown
Row 1: (k1, k2tog, p1, p2 tog) all round, reducing sts by one third. Now continue in the Shallow Zig-zag pattern, but only 2 sts wide:
Row 2: (k2, p2) to end.
Row 3: p1, (k2, p2) to last 2 sts, p2.
Row 4: as row/round 3.
Row 5: (p2, K2) to end.
Row 6: as row/round 5.
Row 7: as row/round 3.
Row 8: as row/round 4.
Continue with 2 sts-wide zig-zag pattern until required length. To help close the center, reduce number of sts by working k2tog, p2tog across the last row.

Break off yarn, leaving a long thread. Use darning needle to thread through all sts and pull tightly to gather. Fasten securely. Sew side seam. Oversew gap at crown or cover with a pom-pom (see page 141).

North Ronaldsay fleece

The multicolored North Ronaldsay—individual sheep and entire flocks vary from white to dark gray, as well as moorit browns—have strong personalities. They tend to scatter, rather than cluster, when threatened and have scant respect for dogs or people. They are (marginally!) easier to manage with a bucket of feed.

As they are so small, with neither rams nor ewes generally exceeding 66 lbs (30 kg), North Ronaldsay sheep have been mainly kept for wool rather than meat. Their fleeces are almost a double coat, like cashmere goats or Icelandic sheep. This means there is a short soft undercoat mixed with a longer, hair coat.

Research suggests today's sheep are little changed from the "original" type, with similar skeletons found on the island of North Ronaldsay in Stone Age settlements.

These sheep are suited to conservation grazing, as they will browse from grass, but also hedges, bushes, and woody plants. It is great to watch these little sheep carefully picking gorse, thistle, or bramble flowers without pricking their lips.

North Ronaldsay sheep also eat seaweed—useful on islands where grass is sparse and there are few trees. Indeed, since 1832 the North Ronaldsay flock has been confined to the island foreshore by a 6-foot (1.8-meter) high dry-stone wall for almost all the year.

Of course, this is a rare breed, classified as Endangered by the Rare Breeds Survival Trust, with less than 500 registered breeding ewes. However, the breed society, which was only established in 1997, has helped to popularize North Ronaldsay sheep and there are now flocks throughout the UK. On the island, the flock manages itself: only those able to withstand the local conditions can survive and breed.

BREED AT A GLANCE

Sheep type: Primitive. Northern, short-tailed.
Appearance: Small, multicolored sheep, both within single sheep and across the flock, ranging from white to dark gray and also browns and fawns. They have neat curling horns on all rams and a few ewes, and hair-less legs.
Rare breeds status: Rare Breeds Survival Trust classification is Endangered.
Further information: UK breed society: www.nrsf.co.uk.
History: Farmed on the Orkney Islands off the north of Scotland for centuries; thought to have been established in the UK around the 9th century, probably by mixing sheep brought by Viking and Saxon raiders with the local (and most likely very similar) sheep.

White DK yarn

mid-gray
Aran yarn

FLEECE FACT FILE
Fleece weight: 3–4 lbs (1.5–2 kg),
but often nearer 2 lbs (1 kg)
Staple length: 1.5–3 in (4–8 cm)
Micron count: 25–40
Crimp: Variable, coarse
Handle: Fine with some kemp
Natural colors: White, pale to dark
gray, browns, and fawns
Mixed colors: Grays
Luster: Slight

White Aran
yarn

dark gray DK
yarn

Close-up of knitted Aran sample

raw fleece

dark gray
Aran yarn

scoured
fleece

carded fleece

North Ronaldsay yarn

In common with Icelandic sheep and cashmere goats, North Ronaldsay sheep have a double coat—a short, soft undercoat mixed with a longer, hair coat. The proportion of soft fibers enables North Ronaldsay yarns to feel much softer than the numbers imply.

In cashmere, it is necessary to remove the coarser hair before spinning the fleece, but doing this with North Ronaldsay, in my view, completely removes the character of the fleece, as the hairs are usually dark and white and add more natural color to the yarns.

These yarns come up naturally quite strongly heathered and can be sorted into shades of white, pale gray, dark gray and brown-gray for spinning. Scouring requires the removal of salt and sand, not common with other sheep!

Owing to the character of the fleece, it works best in thicker yarns, from Double Knitting upwards. It can be over-dyed and felted, but I feel it is too rare for this and prefer to make naturally colored yarns.

The yarns, like the wool, are designed to have structure, lightness and bulk, making ideal warm layers, so we have chosen an airy waistcoat in Aran-weight yarn as a pattern.

YARN USER'S GUIDE
Good for ...
- Spinning
- Felting
- Dyeing
- Weaving

Not so good for ...
- Fine yarns

Due to the multi-colored and heathered nature of the yarn, it does not work as well as more monochrome yarns to show distinct texture in cables or other textured designs. However, North Ronaldsay yarn would also work for the Black Welsh Mountain waistcoat, the Manx Loagthan scarf, mittens, and hat, the Hebridean cushion cover, the Zwartbles cardigan or, combined with other dyed yarns, a version of the Shetland waistcoat. It can also be used for blankets made from squares knitted using different colors.

Paler North Ronaldsay fleeces can be dyed successfully. As it is produced by hardy sheep it is perhaps not surprising that the wool is best used for warm, durable outer garments.

Airy waistcoat

By Myra Mortlock

This smart casual waistcoat comes in two sizes and is worked in three pieces, then joined at the shoulders. It is trimmed with a stylish curled edge at the armholes and neck before finally joining the side seams. The pattern has a garter and moss-stitch panel design and is light and airy to give more warmth. For a more formal and lacier style, knit in Double Knitting worsted-spun yarn, increasing needle size for gauge.

The waistcoat is closed with a toggle or button, but you could use a brooch or shawl pin instead.

Method

BACK

With size 10.5 (6.5 mm) knitting needles, cast on 63 69 sts.
Row 1: (k3, p3) repeat to last 3 sts, k3.
Row 2: (k3, p1, k1, p1) repeat to last 3 sts, k3.
Repeat Row 2 to form pattern. Continue until work measures 10.25 (11) in (26 (28) cm).

Shape armhole
Tip: Slip 1st st of every decrease row to give smooth curve.
Row 1: bind off 3 sts at start of row; work in pattern to end.
Row 2: as row 1.
Row 3: bind off 2 sts at start of row; work in pattern to end.
Row 4: as row 3.
Row 5: bind off 1 st at start of row; work in pattern to end.
Row 6: as row 5.
Work 2 more rows without decreasing.

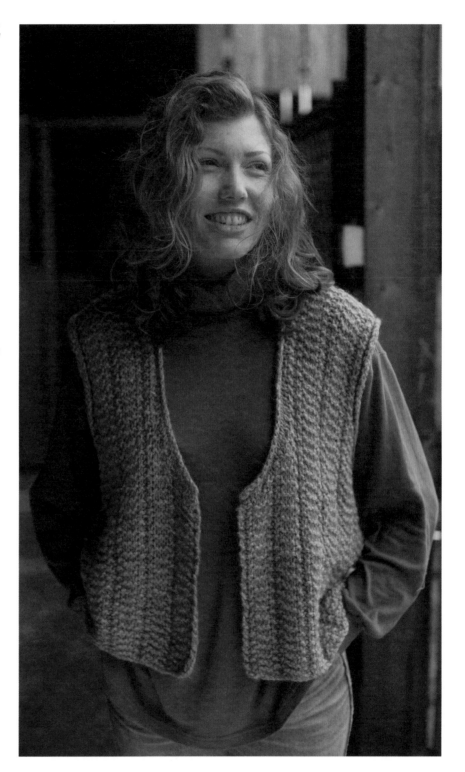

YARN REQUIREMENTS
North Ronaldsay Aran yarn
• Total amount of wool by weight and approximate length:
U.S. size 10-12: 350 g/532 yd (490 m)
U.S. size 14-16: 400 g/608 yd (560 m)

K 2 together at beginning and end of next row.
Repeat these 3 rows twice.
Work 3 rows without shaping.
K 2 tog at beginning and end of next row 43 (49) sts remain.
Continue until work measures 18.5 (20) in (47 (51) cm).

Shape back neck
Work 15 (17) sts and turn.
Next row: at neck edge k2 tog, work to armhole end.

Shape shoulder
Bind off 7 (8) sts. Work return row without shaping.
Bind off remaining sts. Leave center 13 (15) sts on a holder. Finish other shoulder to match.

FRONTS (make 2)

Note: the side seams are offset towards the back, and there is an extra five-stitch decrease on each front underarm.

With size 10.5 (6.5 mm) needles, cast on 36 (39) sts.
Row 1: Smaller size (k3, p3) repeat to end. Larger size (p3, k3) repeat to last 3 sts, p3.
Row 2: Both sizes (p1, k1, p1, k3) repeat to end, larger size, last 3 sts, p1, k1, p1.
Form pattern by repeating garter st and moss st panels as for back.
Continue until piece measures 8.25 (8.5) in (21 (22) cm).

Shape center front opening
(Small size has K3 at center edge of both fronts).
Row 1: Bind off 4 sts; pattern to end.
Row 2: (also row 4, 6 and 8) work without shaping.
Row 3: Bind off 3 sts; work in pattern to end.
Row 5: Bind off 2 sts; work in pattern to end.
Row 7: Bind off 1 st; pattern to end.
Row 9: Bind off 1 st, pattern to end.

SMALL SIZE: at armhole edge bind off 5 sts.
Keeping front edge straight, on next alternate row bind off 3 sts at underarm; following alternate row 2 sts; next alternate row 1 st. Work in pattern on 14 sts until work measures 18.5 in (47 cm).
Bind off 7 sts at shoulder edge. Work one row without shaping.
Bind off remaining sts

LARGE SIZE: continue until piece measures 11 in (28 cm). At armhole edge bind off 5 sts. On next alternate row bind off 3 sts at underarm, following alternate row 2 sts; next alternate row 1 st; next alternate row 1 st. Work in pattern on 16 sts until work measures same as back to shoulder. Bind off 8sts at armhole. Work 1 row. Bind off remaining 6 sts.

Work second front, laying the pieces side by side to check they are a mirror image as you work. Join shoulder seams.

Work armhole facings
RS facing pick up 37 (41) sts from Front underarm to shoulder and 32 (37) sts from shoulder seam to Back underarm. 69 (78) sts.

MEASUREMENTS
Garment bust size: 40 (44) in (102 (112) cm)
Length from base to back neck: 18.5 (20) in (47 (51) cm)
Instructions are given for the smallest size first, followed by large in brackets

NEEDLES & NOTIONS
1 pair size 10.5 (6.5 mm) knitting needles
1 large toggle or decorative button
1 stitch holder or spare knitting needle

GAUGE
Approx 13.5 sts x 10 rows = 4 in (10 cm) over stocking stitch on size 10.5 (6.5 mm) needles
Adjust needle size to give required tension.

SKILL LEVEL	

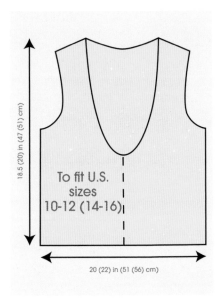

18.5 (20) in (47 (51) cm)

To fit U.S. sizes 10-12 (14-16)

20 (22) in (51 (56) cm)

WS facing: purl. RS facing: knit.
Bind off loosely.

Neck and front facing
RS facing, pick up 37 sts from front edge to shoulder seam, 2 sts from back shaping, 15 sts from holder, 2 sts from other side back shaping and 37 sts to other front edge. 93 sts.
WS facing: purl. RS facing: knit.
Bind off loosely.
Make thread loop and sew on button. Place garment on a cloth, press to shape and cover with a damp cloth. When almost dry transfer to a hanger to allow facings to set.

Romney fleece

The Romney adapted to survive on exposed and isolated salt marshes. This has served them well and they are found across the world—from Portugal to North and South America and the Falkland Islands, New Zealand, and Australia. The UK breed society claims: "The sun never sets on Romney sheep."

The Romney sheep has a large, dense, versatile, longwool fleece with a range of fiber types, from coarse to fine, which differ according to where the animal was bred. For example, the UK micron count is 30–34 on average, but more like 35–37 microns in New Zealand and half-way between these two in the U.S.

The Romney has traveled the world as a pure-bred animal and to crossbreed and create the Perendale, Driesdale, Coopworth, and Corriedale breeds. In New Zealand they supplanted the Merinos to number half the total sheep in the country by the 1850s, rising to three-quarters by 1955. They became the basis of the country's lamb meat trade. The Romney was first imported to the U.S. in 1904.

At present, New Zealand Romneys are being imported into the UK to use as terminal sires for meat breeding. Ewes weigh from 143–187 lbs (65 kg up to 85 kg) and rams from 198–242 lbs (90 kg to 110 kg).

As you might expect, the Romney is not rare, but it comes in many forms. For example, the fleece may be very fine and evenly crimped, or considerably coarser with an indistinct crimp. Although they are generally white, some can be black or brown. There is a flock in southern England, attached to a small worsted-spinning mill, which has Black Romneys, bred pure over several generations.

BREED AT A GLANCE

Sheep type: Medieval longwool.
Appearance: Perhaps the classic medium-large white sheep from children's picture books! The Romney has a bulky, mid-length white semi-luster fleece, no horns, a top-knot, forward pointing ears set on the side of the head and a fat, long tail.
Rare breeds status: None.
Further information:
UK breed society: www.romneysheepuk.com.
U.S. and Canada breed society:
www.americanromney.org.
History: Has grazed the low-lying Romney Marsh in Kent, southeast England, for centuries. They probably gained some genes from Roman imports, but the modern sheep originate from the thirteenth century, although they were "improved" with some Leicester genes in the eighteenth century.

raw fleece

scoured
fleece

carded fleece

FLEECE FACT FILE
Fleece weight: 7–11 lbs (3–5 kg)
Staple length: 4–7 in (10–17 cm)
Micron count: UK average: 30–34, New Zealand average 35–57, US average 30–35
Crimp: Well-defined
Handle: Coarse to fine
Natural colors: White, black, brown
Mixed colors: Browns and grays
Luster: Semi-luster

Close-up of knitted Guernsey sample

5 ply Guernsey yarn

Romney yarn

The considerable variations in Romney yarns—we have found wool as fine and soft as Corriedale, but with the added luster—mean it can be used for many things. While it is ideal for hard-wearing items such as gloves, socks, and jackets, softer wool can be used for garments worn next to the skin. Coarser examples should be used for durable rugs, mats, and chair seats.

The majority of New Zealand Romney wool is used for carpets, providing the bulk and resilience to go with the harder wearing attributes of mountain sheep such as Driesdale in New Zealand or Cheviot and Welsh Mountain in the UK.

The wool is good for hand-spinning and quite easy for beginners, with relatively low lanolin, so it is also easier to wash and has a higher yield than others wools.

We have used a mixed range of British Romney wool to make a 5-ply Guernsey yarn and have also used Romney to make a gray/fawn version of this yarn, blended with Hebridean and Manx Loagthan wool.

Careful selection would enable Romney wool to work from Double Knitting to Chunky yarns and provide soft, bulky warm results, with softer, finer fiber best suited to woolen spinning and the more mixed and coarser fiber better worsted-spun.

Since we are using a 5-ply Guernsey yarn, which is also relatively inelastic and so will not knit up as economically as woolen-spun yarns, the obvious choice is our Guernsey design.

However, these 5-ply yarns can also be used for textured designs on bags, Aran designs (use large needles to make it go further), accessories (use the yarn with three or four strands at a time for the Herdwick designs), or pillows, and could also be considered for socks as this yarn is also hard wearing.

YARN USER'S GUIDE

Good for ...
- Carpets
- Inner or outer garments, depending on the fleece
- Rugs, mats, and pillows
- Dyeing
- Hand-spinning
- Felting

Not so good for ...
- Baby clothes

Romney yarns are ideal for textured knits and this, combined with the resilience of the fibers, makes it ideal for the Guernsey pattern.

Traditional Guernsey pullover

By Sue Blacker

A Guernsey is a traditional sweater worn by fishermen. I have chosen a white Romney yarn because it is probably the easiest to work with for a first-time Guernsey knitter. And, although I have not found any examples, I believe the fishermen of Kent would have worn Guernseys like those from Cornwall, Guernsey, Jersey, Yorkshire, Wales, Ireland, or Scotland.

This is a traditionally knitted and styled Guernsey. They are normally quite close fitting so if you want it loose, make a larger size! However, it is relatively easy to resize Guernseys, and instructions are given for this within the pattern.

The body is worked in the round, then back and forth for the yoke, with the sleeves also knitted in the round, picking up and working downwards from the shoulders, and again finished with a deep rib welt.

Two designs are given for the yoke, one plainer and one more detailed, but you can always continue in stocking stitch (at the risk of terminal boredom?).

Make a traditional submariner's pullover by knitting the garment entirely in stocking stitch and making a polo neck.

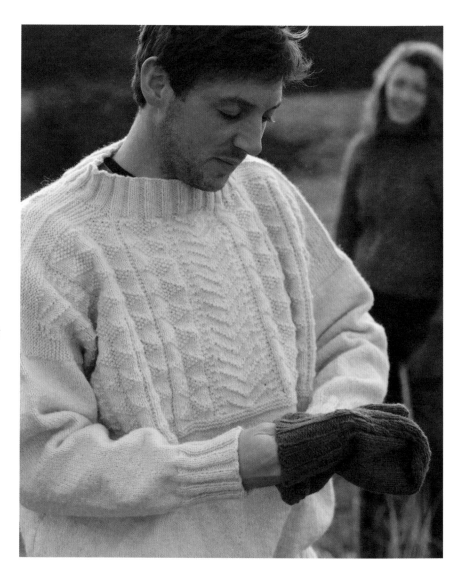

YARN REQUIREMENTS
White Romney 5-ply Guernsey Knitting yarn
• Total amount of wool by weight and approximate length:
Small: 800 g/1,936 yds (1,856 m)
Medium: 900 g/2,178 yds (2,080 m)
Large: 1,000 g/2,420 yds (2,320 m)

Method

BODY (make 1)

Using size 1 (2.25 mm) circular needle, and English/long-tail method, cast on 336 (372, 408) sts. Ensuring the sts are not twisted, join into a round. Work k3, p3 rib for 3 in (8 cm) (or less or more, as preferred).

Increase by 12 sts evenly around the last round to make 348 (384, 420) sts, finishing in line with the cast-on tail.

Mark the side seam lines by purling 1 st at each side of work on each round:
Mark the next st as one side and count around 173 (191, 209) sts to the other side to

make the second mark, so you have 2 sides of 173 (191, 209) sts each, plus 2 seam sts.

TIP: You can make these lines as garter stitch by working one knit and one purl stitch on alternate rounds, so they will show less—but this is more to remember!

Continue in st st (all rounds k sts) until the work measures 14 in (36 cm) (or longer or shorter as preferred).

Begin pattern and gussets
See pages 106–107 for pattern. **Do not start gussets until you have decided on your pattern.**

GUSSETS

The gussets are worked in st st, starting from the side seams and increasing by 2 sts on each gusset, and at each edge of the growing gusset every 4th row. The first increase is made by working into both sides of the seam stitch to make 3 sts from one. Continue the increases for 48 rows to make each gusset 25 sts wide plus 2 seam stitches. The new stitches become seam stitches on either side of the gusset and can be worked in purl or garter stitch to maintain the line. You can include them in the pattern as their position is obvious at this stage. However, once the sleeve has been added there will be a seam stitch to mark where decreases are made on either side, so for the first-time Guernsey knitter, it is worth continuing with seam stitches.

Once you have worked 48 gusset rows the work will measure about 18 in (46 cm) from the cast-on edge, making the gusset about 5 in (12.5 cm) long to its widest point, and the front and back will each still consist of 173 (191, 209) sts.

MEASUREMENTS
Chest: 36 (40, 44) in (92 (102, 112) cm)
Actual chest: 44 (50, 54) in
(112 (128, 142) cm)
Length from shoulder to hem: 27 in (69 cm)
Length from under-arm gussets to hem: 14 in (36 cm)
Yoke length: 13 in (33 cm)
Sleeve seam: 19 in (48 cm)
Instructions are given for the smallest size first, followed by medium and large in brackets).

| SKILL LEVEL | 🧶🧶🧶 |

NEEDLES & NOTIONS
1 pair size 1 (2.25 mm) long, straight needles
1 pair size 1 (2.25 mm) 39 in (100 cm) circular needle
1 set of four size 1 (2.25 mm) double-pointed needles (for narrow section of sleeve)
Cable needle
Stitch markers or colored thread
2 stitch holders or waste yarn

GAUGE
Approx 36 sts x 40 rows = 4 in (10 cm) over stocking stitch on size 1 (2.25 mm) needles.
Adjust needle size to give required tension.
A simple way to increase the size of the garment is to increase the needle size, although this will also reduce the stitch density and therefore the wind-proof characteristics of the final garment (but check your gauge if you plan to do this).
Using size 2 (2.75 mm) needles will give approximately 34 sts and 39 rows to 4 in (10 cm) and add approximately 7 in (18 cm) to the chest size.
Using size 2.5 (3 mm) needles will give approximately 30 sts x 38 rows to 4 in (10 cm) and add approximately 10 in (26 cm) to the chest size.

ABBREVIATIONS (see also page 140)
3 and 3 rib: K3, p3 all rounds when working in the round (circular or double-pointed needles), alternating (k3, p3 on row 1, p3, k3 on row 2) on two needles.
Moss stitch: K1, p1 all rounds, so the knit stitches are over the purl stitches on the previous round when working in the round (circular or double-pointed needles). Alternate rows of k1, p1 on 2 needles.

TIP: You can knit a pattern—such as the initials of the Guernsey owner—into the gusset. Work this out using graph paper, or embroider it later.

Put the gusset stitches onto stitch holders or waste yarn and continue to work the front and back of the sweater separately using a pair of long needles.

NOTE: For both front and back, it is usual to frame the yoke pattern with a "strap" of garter stitch, working 5 sts at each side as knit sts so that the patterned area is arranged over the middle 163 (181, 199) sts. You can

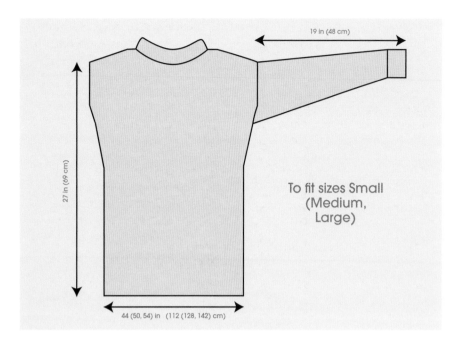

19 in (48 cm)

To fit sizes Small
(Medium,
Large)

27 in (69 cm)

44 (50, 54) in (112 (128, 142) cm)

increase the width of this "strap" to simplify the design, or enlarge the sweater.

The front and back are worked in the same way, in your chosen pattern, until armhole measures 8 in (20 cm) deep.

Divide sts: 58 (64, 70) sts for each shoulder, with 57 (62, 68) sts placed on a stitch holder for the neck.

Shape shoulder
Work each shoulder as 12 rows of garter stitch, decreasing one st at the neck edge on 3rd and 7th rows.

Join each pair of shoulders by grafting or knitting off. To do this, put the sts for both shoulders on two needles held parallel and, using a third needle bind off by working into one stitch from each needle for each bind-off stitch.

Neck
Pick up and knit 162 (174, 184) sts around the neck: 57 (63, 68) from each neck stitch holder and 24 from each shoulder edge. Now work k3, p3 rib for 15 rounds, or depth required.

Sleeves
Using size 1 (2.25 mm) circular needle pick up and knit 132 sts around armhole, plus 2 seam sts and 25 gusset sts. (159 sts).

TIP: At this stage, you can add a decorative band or panel (see pattern options below). A band can start at the end of the gusset, but a sleeve panel should start the moment the sleeve is cast on and be worked over the center sts, with the center of the pattern marked at the 61st stitch when picking up.

Work the remainder of the gusset by decreasing one st at each end of every 4th row until a single seam stitch remains. Transfer to 4 double-pointed needles when the sleeve becomes too narrow to work easily on the circular needle (or use the magic loop method, see page 141). Once the gusset is complete, continue to work the sleeve in st stitch (with or without a pattern band or panel), maintaining the seam stitch.

Decrease 1 st either side of the seam stitch every 4th round

10 times and then every 5th round until 79 sts remain, knitting last 2 sts together (78 sts). Continue in st stitch until sleeve measures 15.5 in (39 cm) or required length. Finish with 3 in (8 cm) of 3 x 3 rib and bind off firmly in rib.

NOTE: Working the sleeves downwards allows you to try the sweater on and adjust the length as you work.

PATTERNS
These designs are all worked over 173 sts, so the garter stitch band at either side is widened or reduced to take up the additional sts in the larger sizes, leaving the design itself in one size. The charts can be found on pages 107 and 108.

SIMPLE GARTER AND CHECKER-BOARD
Although this is simple, it will look quite stylish!
Rounds 1-12: purl all sts to match the shoulder band.
Round 13: start the pattern, reducing by 1 st at gussets: k10 (19, 28), work checker-board pattern over next 153 sts, k10 (19, 28), and repeat for second half of pullover.

Checker-board stitch
Knitting in the round, over 20 rounds:
Rounds 1 to 10: (k9, p9) repeated 17 times, k9.
Rounds 11 to 20: (p9, k9) repeated 17 times, p9.
Once you have completed the gusset, the pattern will be worked on 2 needles, over 12 rows:
Row 1: (K9, p9) repeated 17 times, k9.
Row 2: (p9, k9) repeated 17 times, p9.
Rows 3 to 10: repeat rows 1 and 2 four times more.
Row 11: as row 2.

Row 12: as row 1.
Rows 13-20: repeat rows 11 and 12 four times more.

NOTE: An alternative to checker board stitch, with more depth and ridges between the checks, is the Vicar of Morwenstowe slate pattern from Mary Wright's *Cornish Knit Frocks and Guernseys*, **which is worked over 28 rounds. You could also consider the Lizard Lattice, over 51 rounds, or Polperro Laughing Boy, over 8 rounds.**

Simple variations or additions
- Work a 6st cable either side of your checker-board. Reduce the garter-stitch edges by 12 sts each side and work as follows:
- **In the round:** rounds 1-5 are k1, p2, k6, p2, k1 before and after the checker board, then round 6 is k1, p2, C6F, p2, k1 and k1, p2, C6B, p2, k1 respectively at either side (so that the cables are symmetrical).
- **Using 2 needles:** rows 1and 3 are k1, p2, k6, p2, k1. Row 5 is k1, p2, C6F, p2, k1 and k1,p2, C6B, p2, k1 respectively at either side of the checker board and rows 2, 4 and 6 are p1, k2, p6, k2, p1.
- Work 2–3 pairs of twisted rib sts either side of your checker board: reduce the garter edges by 12 sts each side and work T2, p2, T2, p2, T2, p2 each round, or with 2 needles the RS rows will be p2, k2, p2, k2, p2, k2.

Traditional Guernsey pattern
These patterns are all in knit and purl with no cables. Use the charts to help you to follow this. On 2 needles, the even-numbered rounds will have the k and p sts reversed to work in st stitch. Two patterns are given:
- **Chevrons** with moss stitch panels between, worked over 23 sts and 8 rows. This can be done across 161 sts to make 7 chevrons, so you will need to work 6 (15, 24) sts for the garter stitch edges.
- **Moss stitch diamonds** on a st stitch background with garter stitch panels between each, worked over 15 sts and 12 rows. This can be worked across 165 sts to make 11 diamonds. The garter stitch panels will need to be 4 (13, 22) sts wide.
- These patterns may also be used together and worked as horizontal bands. For example, work a garter stitch ridge of 6 rows, followed by a band of diamonds over 12 rows, then 6 more rows of garter stitch, then work the rest of the yoke in chevrons. To keep the garter stitch edges even omit first and last garter sts on the diamond band.
- You will have around 120 rows for the yoke design in total, including the 12 rows of garter stitch at the shoulder and possibly 12 rows as a band from which to launch your pattern. This would therefore be 12 repeats of chevrons or 8 repeats of diamonds.

Other variations
You can also combine these patterns vertically (see photograph on page 104):
- 1 chevron, 3 diamonds, 1 chevron, 3 diamonds, 1 chevron over 159 sts, with garter stitch panels 7 (16, 25) sts wide.
- 2 diamonds, 2 chevrons, 1 diamond, 2 chevrons, 2 diamonds, over 167 sts, with garter stitch edges 3 (12, 21) sts wide.
- Alternate 1 diamond, then 1 chevron, four times, finishing with another diamond, making 167 sts, with garter stitch edges 3 (12, 21) sts wide.
- 3 diamonds, 3 chevrons, then 3 diamonds, making 159 sts, with garter stitch panels 7 (16, 25) sts wide.
- 1 diamond, 5 chevrons,

Chevron pattern

	1	2	3	4	5	6	7	8	9	10	11	12	13	14	15	16	17	18	19	20	21	22	23
8					x														x				
7		x	x			x												x			x	x	
6							x									x							
5	x					x								x									x
4					x								x										
3		x	x					x				x								x	x		
2									x		x												
1	x				x					x									x			x	

KEY

x p on RS; k on WS   □ k on RS; p on WS

Stiches for chevron pattern
Round 1 P1, k2, p1, k7, p1, k7, p1, k2, p1.
Round 2 K10, p1, k1, p1, k10
Round 3 K1, p2, k6, p1, k3, p1, k6, p2, k1.
Round 4 K8, p1, k5, p1, k8.
Round 5 P1, k6, p1, k7, p1, k6, p1.
Round 6 K6, p1, k9, p1, k6.
Round 7 K1, p2, k2, p1, k11, p1, k2, p2, k1.
Round 8 K4, p1, k13, p1, k4.

Chevron pattern with repeats

KEY
☒ p on RS; k on WS   ☐ k on RS; p on WS

Moss diamond pattern

	1	2	3	4	5	6	7	8	9	10	11	12	13	14	15
12								x							
11	x						x	x							x
10						x	x	x							
9	x			x		x	x	x		x					x
8				x	x	x	x	x	x						
7	x		x	x	x	x	x	x	x	x	x				x
6				x	x	x	x	x	x						
5	x			x		x	x	x		x					x
4						x	x	x							
3	x						x	x							x
2								x							
1	x														x

KEY
☒ p on RS; k on WS   ☐ k on RS; p on WS

Stiches for moss diamond pattern

Round 1   P1, k13, p1.
Round 2   K7, p1, k7.
Round 3   P1, k5, p1, k1, p1, k5, p1.
Round 4   K5, p1, k1, p1, k1, p1, k5.
Round 5   P1, k3, p1, k1, p1, k1, p1, k1, p1, k3, p1.
Round 6   K3, p1, k1, p1, k1, p1, k1, p1, k1, p1, k3.K2, p2, k2, P3,
Round 7   k1, p1, k1, p1, k1, p1, k1, p1, k1, p1, k1, p1, k1, p1.
Round 8   K3, p1, k1, p1, k1, p1, k1, p1, k1, p1, k3.
Round 9   P1, k3, p1, k1, p1, k1, p1, k1, p1, k3, p1.
Round 10 K5, p1, k1, k1, k1, p1, k5.
Round 11 P1, k5, p1, k1, p1, k5, p1.
Round 12 K7, p1, k7.

---

1 diamond, making 145 sts, with garter stitch panels of 14 (23, 32) sts or make a stronger vertical line each side of the diamonds. These are all symmetrical, and add to an odd number of sts, allowing the garter stitch edges to be the same on both sides.

Adding patterns to the sleeves
When knitting down the sleeves, you may wish to work a band of diamonds, bordered with garter stitch, or a simple garter stitch border, or the checkerboard pattern. Normally a sleeve pattern will stop at the end of the gusset, so you have around 40-50 rows to play with while tapering the gusset.

On a traditional fisherman's sweater, the rest of the sleeve would be plain. As an alternative, work a central vertical line of diamonds to the cuff. Or, if you have used cables on the yoke, try a cable with a narrow reverse st stitch border.

Moss pattern with repeats

KEY
☐ p on RS; k on WS
☐ k on RS; p on WS

Ryeland fleece

The Ryeland is a "typical" sheep. Being small and gentle (and short legs make it harder to leap over fences), they are a favorite among smallholders and are also sought after for their meat. As they have a tendency to put on weight if fed concentrates or on rich pastures, they are also good for sparse pastures and a total grass diet and consequently work well under organic husbandry.

The Ryeland has been famous since the Middle Ages for its fine wool. The abundant fleece is well-suited for making clothes. It is said Queen Elizabeth I was so fond of her "Lemster" wool stockings that she insisted on all her wool stockings being from Ryeland wool (although she quickly developed a taste for silk stockings!).

The sheep are a small, short-wooled version of the white, fat-tailed sheep so are no doubt distantly related to Roman imports and Romneys rather than to northern short-tailed sheep. The ewes weigh 110–132 lbs (50–60 kg) and rams 165–176 lbs (75–80 kg).

A breed society was formed in 1903 to try to ensure the survival of these sheep, which were not competing well with the more commercial Leicester-based breeds.

Having the help of a breed society did not ensure success for the Ryeland sheep, and by the 1970s it was again facing a decline. In 1973, with less than 500 registered breeding ewes The Rare Breeds Survival Trust found Ryeland sheep to be Endangered, however, today with 3,000 registered breeding ewes they are now classified as a Native Breed. This success is partly due to the popularity of the Ryeland in small flocks, and also the attractions of its white and colored downland wool and encouragement of the development of the Colored Ryeland, which has no white genes and so will consistently breed colored progeny.

BREED AT A GLANCE

Sheep type: Native.

Appearance: Ryelands are small, with dense, short, white fleece, a slightly compact and tubby appearance, no horns, short woolly legs, dark feet, and something of the teddy bear in general style. Ryelands can also come in a colored version, which is a lovely brown-gray.

Rare breeds status: None.

Further information:
UK breed society: www.ryelandfbs.com.

History: The Ryeland is said to have been specifically developed in the twelfth century by the monks at Leominster near Hereford, on the borderlands between England and Wales, to make fine wool for cloth. They were also used to graze land where rye was being grown, to stimulate the growth, hence the name.

carded fleece

mid 4-ply yarn

dark Aran yarn

scoured fleece

light Aran yarn

mid DK yarn

pale DK yarn

FLEECE FACT FILE
Fleece weight: 4–5 lbs (2–2.75 kg)
Staple length: 3–4 in (7.5–10 cm)
Micron count: 28–32
Crimp: Fine
Handle: Soft
Natural colors: White, black, gray, brown
Mixed colors: Grays and browns
Luster: High

dark DK yarn

dark 4-ply yarn

raw fleece

Close-up of knitted DK sample

Ryeland yarn

Ryeland is typical downland wool, being short, resilient, stretchy, and with good insulating properties. It has little kemp, though this may be colored in the white sheep, and the crimp is indistinct. Do not, however, try felting it as you could spend a long time not getting a result!

White and Colored Ryeland wools are very similar and can be spun alone or mixed to create an intermediate shade of yarn. The Colored wool, which is mainly gray but with brown highlights, is particularly attractive and makes a beautiful heathered yarn. The white wool is one of the creamiest in color of all the white wools, being similar to that of Blue-faced Leicester sheep. It is often woven to make good tweeds and rugs.

Despite its reputation with Queen Elizabeth I and her fine stockings, Ryeland's bouncy downland wool means that nowadays it is better suited to woollen spun thicker yarns, Double Knitting and above, and works well for outer garments. Because it does not felt easily, it will also retain the stitch definition in cabled and textured garments over years of wear. Selection for finer wool in small flocks will reduce the micron count and make for softer yarns.

We have chosen Ryeland for a child's jacket. This is worked in two strands, so it is possible to consider using one each of white, mid-colored, or colored Ryeland yarn to make a paler or darker tweedy version. Ryeland yarn will also work for the patterns we have provided for Black Welsh Mountain, Galway, Hebridean, Jacob, Manx Loagthan, or Zwartbles yarns.

Soft and airy, Ryeland yarn is also resilient, making it perfect for textured stitches and cable designs that will retain their shape after wear and washing.

YARN USER'S GUIDE

Good for ...
- Clothing
- Dyeing
- Textured stitches and cables
- Tweeds
- Rugs

Not so good for ...
- Felting

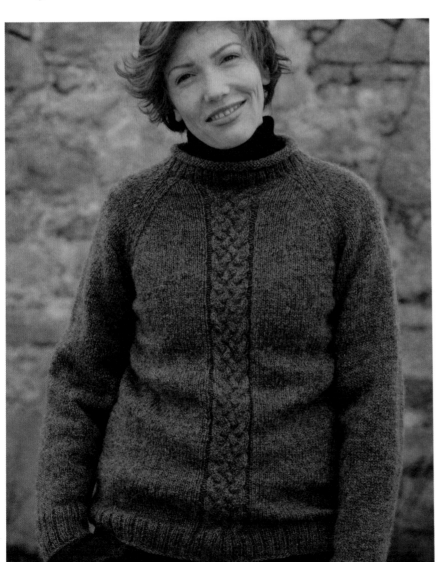

Ryeland child's hooded jacket

by Myra Mortlock
and Sue Blacker

This textured jacket is perfect to wear outdoors on a chilly fall day. It is knitted using two strands of Ryeland yarn in stocking stitch, while seeds of purl stitches add visual interest. The seed stitches are continued on to the edges of the garment and are a simple way to add texture to the fabric.

You can use one color of yarn, or choose one strand of white and one of colored for a tweedy effect.

The loop fastening means there is no need to knit buttonholes, and you can use buttons or toggles. Finish the hood with a tassel, or replace it with a small collar.

YARN REQUIREMENTS

Ryeland worsted-weight/DK

• Total amount of wool by weight and approximate length
Small: 500 g/1,190 yds (1,110 m)
Large: 700 g/1,666 yds (1,540 m)
• Yarn used doubled throughout. Use a single color throughout, or equal amounts of two different colors for a tweedy effect.

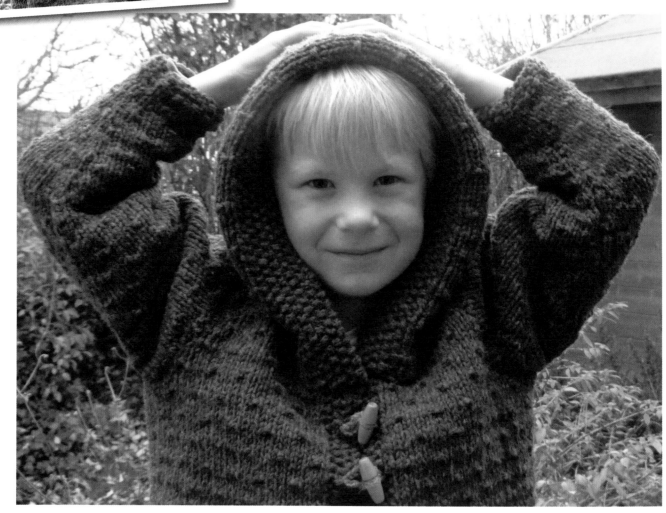

Method

NOTE: working with two strands of yarn is easy, but occasionally you will only pick up one, so check each row. You will usually find the mistake on the next row. Use a crochet hook to pick up and link in the extra strand.

BACK (make 1)

Using size 9 (5.5 mm) needles and 2 strands of yarn together, cast on 50 (60) sts.
Welt pattern:
Row 1: K1, p1, repeat to end.
Row 2: P1 (wool back, slip 1 knitwise, wool forward p1), repeat to last st, k1.
Row 3: as row 1.
Row 4: as row 2, but for larger size increase by 1 st at each end of row 50 (62) sts.
Begin main pattern.

Main pattern
Row 1: Knit.
Row 2: Purl.
Row 3: K3 *p1, k3*, repeat from * to* to last 3 sts, p1, k2.
Row 4: Purl.
Row 5: Knit.
Row 6: Purl.
Row 7: K5 *p1, k3*, repeat from * to* to last st, k1.
Row 8: Purl.
Repeat rows 1-8 until work measures 9.5 (11.5) in

(24 (26) cm).
Shape raglan
Right side facing, continue to knit pattern while decreasing sts as follows:
Row 1: bind off 2 sts, work to end.
Row 2: bind off 2 sts, purl to end.
Row 3: K2 tog, work in pattern to last 2 sts, k2 tog.
Row 4: Purl.
Repeat rows 3 and 4 until 37 (44) sts remain.
Decrease at each end of every row until 15 (18) sts remain.
Bind off.

FRONTS (make 2)

Using size 9 (5.5 mm) needles and 2 strands of yarn together, cast on 26 (32) sts.
Work 4 rows of welt as given for back.
Work seed stitch band of 5 sts at center edge of both fronts (first row k1, p1, second row p1, k1), continuing in main pattern for rest of row until work measures 9.5 (11.5) in (24 (26) cm).

Shape raglan
At side edge bind off 5 (6) sts.
Work one row without shaping.
Decrease one st at side edge on next and following alternate rows to 19 (23) sts.

Shape neck
At neck edge, bind off 5 (6) sts.

Decrease 1 st at both ends of every alternate row until 4 sts remain.
Next row: K2 tog twice.
Next row: K2 tog and bind off last st.
Repeat to make second side, reversing shaping.

SLEEVES (make 2)

Using size 9 (5.5 mm) needles and 2 strands of yarn together, cast on 26 (31) sts.
Work welt as for back.
Change to pattern and work first 4 rows.
Row 5: K1, increase in the next st, work in pattern to the last 2 sts, increase in next st, k1.
Row 6: purl.
Row 7: Work pattern row.
Row 8: purl.
Row 9: increase at both ends as row 5.
Row 10: purl.
Repeat rows 7-10 until work measures 9.5 (11.5) in (24 (26) cm) and you have a total of 46 (55) sts.

Shape raglan
Maintaining pattern, decrease as follows:
Row 1: right side facing, bind off 2 sts, work to end.
Row 2: bind off 2 sts, work to end.
Decrease at each end of every row to 12 (14) sts, then alternate rows to 10 (12) sts.
Bind off.

HOOD (make 1)

The hood is worked as one piece, and follows the main pattern with a band of seed st along the edge. You start knitting at one corner of the neck and work up and over the head, with a center-back seam.

Using size 9 (5.5 mm) needles and 2 strands of yarn together, cast on 6 (8) sts.

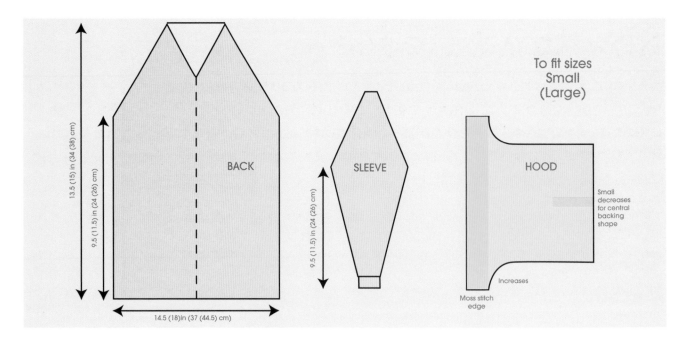

To fit sizes
Small
(Large)

BACK

SLEEVE

HOOD

Small decreases for central backing shape

Increases

Moss stitch edge

13.5 (15) in (34 (38) cm)

9.5 (11.5) in (24 (26) cm)

9.5 (11.5) in (24 (26) cm)

14.5 (18)in (37 (44.5) cm)

Row 2: K1, k twice into next st. (p1, k1) to end.
Row 3: K1, p1, k1, p1, k1, purl to end of row.
Row 4: (Knit row) continue, increasing one st at start of this and alternate rows to 14 (17) sts, introducing main 8-row pattern and maintaining 6 st seed stitch edging.

Back/side neck edge
Cast on another 18 (22) sts.
Work 6 rows in pattern.
At center-back edge, increase 1 st at start of next row.
Work 5 rows, until work measures approximately 3 (4) in (8 (10) cm) from neck edge cast on.
At center back, increase 1 st at start of next row.
Continue in pattern to 17 (20) in (43 (52) cm) from 18 (22) st cast on.
Next row: at center back edge k1, k2 tog. Work to end of row.
Work 5 rows, then repeat decrease.
Work 6 rows.
Next row: at center back edge bind off 18 (22) sts.
Work one row.
Decrease on alternate rows to match other side of hood.
Bind off last 6 (8) sts.

MAKE UP

For general advice on making up garments see page 141.
With wrong sides facing, pin or tack shoulders together and then sew. Fit sleeves to armholes and then sew side and sleeve seams.
Fold hood in half, pin center join on wrong side and sew. Pin center back of hood to center back of body. Pin or tack lower hood edge to body and sew. If liked, fold hood edge inwards and sew down lightly.
Sew toggles on appropriate side for boy or girl.
Make five lengths of l-cord—a knitted tube—for the loops and attach to meet toggles.
To make an l-cord, using two size 9 (5.5 mm) double-pointed needles, cast on 3 sts and k one row. Move the stitches to the opposite end of the needle and knit again, pulling the yarn across the back of the work to close the tube. Repeat until required length. Bind off.
To make a tassel for the hood, cut a piece of card 6.5 in (16 cm) wide. Take two strands of yarn and wind them around the card ten times. Do not cut yarn. Tie start end of yarn to working end. Turn card over and cut

threads opposite the tie. Bind yarn around threads to make tassel. Sew through tassel and secure. Attach tassel to hood.

ADJUSTING THE SIZE OF THE JACKET

You can make the jacket longer in the body or sleeves, but you will need more yarn.
• **To make the jacket larger overall,** knit on one size larger needles, but note that this will result in a looser and less wind-proof version.
• **To make the jacket wider,** you will need to adjust the raglan sleeve and neck edge. To do this, add stitches in groups of 6, allowing 2 for the first part of the decreases (2 extra rows), 2 for the second part (one extra row) and leaving 2 extra at the end, which creates 3 extra rows in length. This will give around 2 in (5 cm) per 6 stitches. If adding more, increase the number decreased in the first two rows of the raglan shaping. You can also add stitches all the way up, to increase the size of the neck. An easier way to enlarge the front is to make the seed stitch bands 6 stitches wider.

Shetland fleece

Shetland sheep have evolved to survive the harsh environment of the islands where they have traditionally been farmed. Shetland wool is either from the breed, from sheep farmed on the Shetland Islands, or sometimes from both! Today organic pedigree Shetland sheep on the Islands have European Union denomination of origin status.

Shetland fleece is a non-luster, fine, soft, and silky wool with a distinctly tiny, dense crimp. Some fleeces can be matted if shorn late, and the sheep can begin to shed them unless shorn on time.

Its Viking heritage can been found in the Norsk nomenclature for fleece colors and markings. The best-known names of the colors are the moorit brown and katmogit or gulmogit (Mouflon markings) grays. There are eleven main colors and thirty five markings, but in 1996 a Shetland Sheep Society survey found sufficient variations to provide a poster of sixty three of these markings.

Adult sheep weigh in at 77–88 lbs (35–40 kg) for ewes and 99–121 lbs (45–55 kg) for rams on the mainland, but as little as 48.4 lbs (22 kg) for a ewe on the Islands.

The Shetland Flockbook society was established in 1927 in Shetland to protect the purity of the breed. The Shetland Sheep Society was set up for the same purpose on the mainland in 1985.

Some Shetland sheep work on conservation grazing in the UK. The breed has been imported into North America.

The Rare Breeds Survival Trust classified Shetland sheep as Endangered in 1977, but by 2008 there were over 800 registered ewes and nearly 300 rams. Today, breeders are focusing on ensuring that the variety of markings is preserved.

BREED AT A GLANCE

Sheep type: Primitive.

Appearance: One of Britain's smallest sheep. The rams usually have curling horns, but the ewes usually do not. They come in a wide variety of colors, which have been the basis of the Fair Isle knitting. Each color and marking pattern has its own Norse name.

Rare breeds status: Native in UK. Recovering in U.S.

Further information: UK breed society: www.shetland-sheep.org.uk. Shetland Flock Book breed society: www.shetland-sheep.co.uk. North American breed society: www.shetland-sheep.org.

History: A hardy, self-sufficient northern short-tailed sheep with Viking ancestry dating back to the eighth century on the Shetland Islands off the coast of Scotland. They have mainly been farmed on the highlands and islands, or on parklands for their attractive appearance.

scoured fleece

raw fleece

FLEECE FACT FILE
Fleece weight: 2.2 lbs (1 kg)
Staple length: 2–4 in (5–10 cm), average 3.5 in (8 cm)
Micron count: Varies from 12 microns at the neck to nearer 30 microns on the rump
Crimp: Tiny, dense
Handle: Fine, soft, and silky
Natural colors: White, gray, beige, moorit, and brown—11 shades in all
Mixed colors: Grays, beiges, and browns
Luster: None

DK dark yarn

4-ply mid yarn

DK pale yarn

Close-up of knitted DK sample

Aran dark yarn

carded fleece

DK mid yarn

4-ply dark yarn

Aran light yarn

Shetland yarn

Like the colors and markings, Shetland fleeces can vary considerably between different animals and within a single fleece. This diversity makes them very interesting for hand-spinning. It is also possible to achieve both a lace-weight yarn and a thicker yarn from the same fleece.

Shetland sheep may once have had a double coat like the North Ronaldsay but now have a single coat of very fine fleece, although it can vary significantly from only 12 microns at the neck to nearer 30 microns on the rump.

The fine wool from Shetland sheep was originally used mainly to knit stockings, exported to the UK and the Netherlands from the seventeenth century onwards. Shetland lace-work shawls—including the famous ring shawls that are so fine they will pass through a wedding ring—were also an export until the early twentieth century, when Fair Isle pullovers, hats, and mittens began to take over.

The wool is versatile, ideal for lace-weight or chunky yarns, soft fabrics, or more solid tweeds, and of course you have generally at least five and possibly up to eleven natural colors. The wool does also dye and felt quite well, so it is better for color work than for textured knitting.

We have chosen a fine scarf and a patterned waistcoat to illustrate the versatility of Shetland wool.

You could also use Shetland yarns for non-luster versions of the Blue-faced Leicester blanket or the Gotland beret patterns, the Manx Loagthan accessories, or the North Ronaldsay or Ryeland designs.

Shetland yarns were used for the original, colorful Fair Isles designs, but the natural shades offer plenty of variety to the knitter. The yarn—from laceweight to Aran—is sturdy but of varying softness so not all will be suitable for childrens' clothes.

Shetland spot waistcoat

by Sasha Kagan

This classic retro style was originally designed by Sasha in the 1970s, but is just as easy to wear now! The original pattern has been updated and adapted for Blacker Yarns 4-ply yarns. Relaxed and casual or stylish, you can dress it up or down happily. The four pockets are a nice feature but all of them or just the upper ones can be omitted if you wish. The back is worked in a neat stretchy twisted rib to fit snugly, so you can wear it as part of a suit as well. The fronts are worked in the Fair Isle design and all the borders are added afterwards, as are the pocket borders and linings.

DESIGNER PROFILE

Sasha Kagan is a name synonymous with the renaissance in contemporary British knitwear. She has been designing and making knitwear since the 1960s and is renowned for her lively use of color and distinctive patterns.

YARN REQUIREMENTS

Pure Shetland wool 4-ply yarn
• Total amount of wool by weight and approximate length:
200 (250, 250, 300, 300) g/760 (950, 950, 1,140, 1,140) yd (700 (875, 875, 1,050, 1,050) m Shetland Dark (A)
50 g/190 yd (175 m) Shetland Moorit
50 g/190 yd (175 m) Shetland Fawn
50 g/190 yd (175 m) Classic Turquoise
50 g/190 yd (175 m) Classic Purple

MEASUREMENTS
Around the bust: 34 (36, 38, 40, 42) in (86 (91, 96, 101, 106) cm)
Garment bust measurement: 36 (38, 40, 42, 44) in (91 cm (96, 101, 106, 111) cm)
Length: 23 (23, 23, 24, 24) in (58 (58, 58, 61, 61) cm)
Instructions are given for the smallest size first, followed by larger sizes brackets

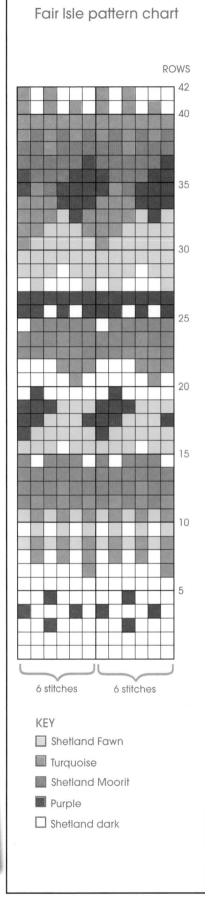
NEEDLES & NOTIONS
One pair each size 1 (2.25 mm), 2 (2.75 mm), 3 (3 mm) needles
Five ¾ in (2 cm) buttons

GAUGE
Approx 27 sts x 29 rows = 4 in (10 cm) over chart pattern on size 3 (3 mm) needles
Approx 32 sts x 26 rows = 4 in (10 cm) over twisted rib pattern on size 1 (2.25 mm) needles
Adjust needle size to give required tension.

ABBREVIATIONS (see also page 140)
Twisted rib: Row 1 (RS): *k1-b, p1* repeat to end. Row 2: k1, P1-b* repeat to end.

Fair Isle pattern chart

ROWS

42
40

35

30

25

20

15

10

5

6 stitches   6 stitches

KEY
☐ Shetland Fawn
▨ Turquoise
▨ Shetland Moorit
▪ Purple
☐ Shetland dark

To fit sizes Extra Small (Small, Medium, Large, Extra Large)

36 (38, 40, 42, 44) in (91 (96, 101, 106, 111) cm)

23 (23, 23, 24, 24) in (58 (58, 58, 61, 61) cm)

Method

BACK (work one)

Using size 1 (2.25 mm) needles and A cast on 122 (130, 140, 150, 158) sts. Work in twisted rib, at the same time increase 1 st at both ends of 8th row, then every following 6th row until there are 144 (152, 162, 172, 180) sts, keeping rib correct.
Continue without shaping until work measures 9 (9, 9, 9.5, 9.5) in (23 (23, 23, 24, 24) cm) from cast on edge.

Shape armholes

Bind off 9 (10, 10, 11, 11) sts at beginning of next 2 rows. Then decrease 1 st at both ends of next and every alt row until 110 (112, 116, 118, 120) sts remain. Continue without further shaping until work measures 17.75 (17.75, 17.75, 18.75, 18.75) in (45 (45, 45, 47, 47.5) cm).

Shape shoulders

Bind off 12 sts at beginning of next 6 rows. Bind off remaining 38 (38, 42, 44, 46) sts.

RIGHT FRONT
(work one)

Using size 3 (3 mm) needles and A cast on 2 sts. Refer to chart and repeat the 42 rows to end. Start chart on sts 1 and 2, adding more of chart at start and end of rows as sts increase.

Extra Small

Row 1: K twice into first st, K1.
Row 2: P3.
Row 3: Knit, increasing 1 st in first st and last st (5 sts).
Repeat rows 3 and 4 five times.
Row 15: K, increasing 1 st in first st and last st (35 sts).
Row 16: Cast on 2 sts, p to end.
Row 17-28: Repeat rows 15 and 16 six times (61 sts).
Row 29: K across row.
Row 30: Cast on 2 sts, p to end (63 sts).

Small

Work rows 1 to 3 as for Extra Small.
Row 4: Cast on 3 sts, p to last 2 sts, increase in next st, p1 (9 sts).
Rows 5-10: repeat rows 3 and 4 three times (27 sts).
Row 11: K, increasing 1 st in first st and last st.
Row 12: cast on 2 sts, p to end.
Rows 13-30: repeat rows 11 and 12 nine times (67 sts).

Medium

Work rows 1 to 4 as for Small.
Rows 5-14: repeat rows 3 and 4 five times (39 sts).
Row 15: K, increase 1 st in first st and last st.
Row 16: cast on 2 sts, p to end.
Rows 17-30: repeat rows 15 and 16 seven times (71 sts).

Large

Work rows 1 to 4 as for Small.
Rows 5-16: repeats rows 3 and 4 six times (45 sts).
Row 17: K, increasing 1 st in first st and last st.
Row 18: cast on 2 sts, p to end.
Rows 19-30: repeat rows 17 and 18 six times (73 sts).

Extra Large

Work rows 1 to 4 as for Small.
Rows 5-20: repeat rows 3 and 4 eight times (57 sts).
Row 21: K, increasing 1 st in first st and last st.
Row 22: cast on 2 sts, p to end.
Rows 23-30: repeat rows 21 and 22 four times (77 sts)

All sizes

Work in pattern for 3 in (7.5 cm) ending with a WS row.

Work lower pocket

Next Row: K18 (20, 22, 23, 25) sts, bind off 27 sts, k to end.
Next row: P18 (20, 22, 23, 25) sts, cast on 27 sts, p to end.
Continue in pattern, increasing 1 st at end of first row (RS) and 22nd row after pocket rows. 65 (69, 73, 75, 79) sts.
Continue until straight edge at center front measures 7 (7, 7, 8, 8) in (17.5 (17.75, 17.75, 20.5, 20.5) cm) ending on WS row.

Shape front neck edge

Decrease 1 st at neck on next and every 5th row 14 (14, 15, 16, 17) times. Continue until work measures 8 (8, 8, 8.5, 8.5) in (20.5 (20.5, 20.5, 21.5, 21.5) cm) at side edge, ending on RS row.

Shape armholes

Bind off 6 (7, 7, 8, 8) sts, p to end. Work 1 row then dec 1 st at beginning of next and every following alternate row 19 (21, 24, 24, 27) times.
When work measures 8.5 (8.5, 8.5, 9, 9) in (21.5 (21.5, 21.5, 23, 23) cm) along side edge, ending with WS row, work Upper Pocket as for Lower Pocket, directly above Lower Pocket.

Continue in pattern until work measures 16.75 (16.75, 16.75, 17.75, 17.75) in (42.5 (42.5, 42.5, 45, 45) cm) ending with RS row

Shape shoulder

Bind off 8 (9, 9, 9, 9) sts at start of next row. Work 1 row.

Bind off 9 sts at start of next and following alternate row.

LEFT FRONT
(work one)
Using size 3 (3 mm) needles and A cast on 2 sts. Refer to chart and repeat the 42 rows to end. Start chart on sts 1 and 2, adding more of chart at beginning and end as you increase. Work shaping at bottom as follows:

Extra Small
Row 1: K twice into first st, k1.
Row 2: P3.
Row 3: K, increasing 1 st in first st and last st (5 sts).
Row 4: P1, inc in next st, p to end, cast on 2 sts (8 sts).
Row 5-14: Repeat rows 3 and 4 five times (33 sts).
Row 15: K, increasing 1 st in first st and last st.
Row 16: P to end, cast on 2 sts.
Row 17-28: Repeat rows 15 and 16 six times (61 sts).
Row 29: K across row.
Row 30: P to end, cast on 2 sts (63 sts).

Small
Work rows 1 to 3 as for Extra Small.
Row 4: P1, increase in next st, p to end, cast on 3 sts (9 sts).
Rows 5-10: repeat rows 3 and 4 three times (27 sts).
Row 11: K, increasing 1 st in first st and last st.
Row 12: P to end, cast on 2 sts.
Rows 13-30: repeat rows 11 and 12 nine times (67 sts).

Medium
Work rows 1 to 4 as for Small.
Rows 5-14: repeat rows 3 and 4 five times (39 sts).
Row 15: K, increase 1 st in first st and last st.
Row 16: P to end, cast on 2 sts.
Rows 17-30: repeat rows 15 and 16 seven times (71 sts).

Large
Work rows 1 to 4 as for Small.

Rows 5-16: repeats rows 3 and 4 six times (45 sts).
Row 17: K, increasing 1 st in first st and last st.
Row 18: P to end, cast on 2 sts.
Rows 19-30: repeat rows 17 and 18 six times (73 sts).

Extra Large
Work rows 1 to 4 as for Small.
Rows 5-20: repeat rows 3 and 4 eight times (57 sts).
Row 21: K, increasing 1 st in first st and last st.
Row 22: P to end, cast on 2 sts.
Rows 23-30: repeat rows 21 and 22 four times (77 sts).

Complete as for right front, reversing shaping and pocket placements.

FINISHING
Darn loose ends into own colors. Block all pieces and press lightly on WS avoiding ribbing. Join shoulder seams.

FRONT BORDERS
(make one)
Borders start at point at bottom of left front and extend to point at bottom of right front. Measure as you work—it should fit snugly when stretched slightly.

Using size 1 (2.25 mm) needles and A cast on 2 sts.
Work k1, p1 twisted rib casting on 2 sts at beginning of every alternate row until 12 sts. Continue until start of straight front edge on right front.
Next row: Rib 4 bind off 3 sts for buttonhole, rib 5.
Next row: Rib 5, cast on 3 sts, rib 4.
Mark 4 more buttonholes on right front—one at point where neckline shaping starts 3 evenly between. Continue in rib, making buttonholes and until border fits up right side of neck around and down other side, ending at corner of peak.

Starting at edge where shaping at beginning finished, bind off 2 sts at beginning of next and every alt row until 2 sts remain. Bind off.

LOWER-EDGE BORDER
(make 2)
Using size 1 (2.25 mm) needles and A cast on 2 sts.
Work in k1 p1 twisted rib casting on 2 sts at beginning of every alt row until there are 12 sts. Continue in rib until border fits from front point to side seam. Bind off.

ARMHOLE BORDERS
(work two)
Using size 1 (2.25 mm) needles, with RS facing and A, pick up and k 1 st for each row on front armhole up to shoulder, then the same number of sts down back armhole. Work 6 rows in k1 p1 twisted rib. Bind off in rib.

POCKET BORDERS
(work four)
Using size 1 (2.25 mm) needles, with RS facing and A, pick up and k 26 sts from bottom edges of pocket slits. Work 6 rows in k1, p1 twisted rib. Bind off in rib.

POCKET LININGS
(work four)
Using size 2 (2.75 mm) needles, with RS facing and A, pick up and K sts across top of pocket slits. Work 2.5 in (6 cm) in st st. Bind off.

MAKING UP
Sew down the edges of pocket borders and linings. Join lower edge borders to front borders and points. Sew front borders. Join side seams, making sure the lower edge of the border is sewn to the back at the base. Attach buttons.

Shetland feather and fan scarf

by Rita Taylor

This scarf is worked in an easy but very attractive lace design called Feather and Fan, which is deservedly one of the most popular lace patterns. It only uses one row of pattern plus three further rows all in knit stitch for a four-row repeat, so it is excellent for beginners. In softest Double Knitting Shetland yarn, the scarf is quick to make and goes back to Shetland lace roots with a modern update of a ribbed middle section to fit cosily with less bulk around the neck. It is worked in two pieces and grafted together to make the ends match perfectly.

Method

First section
Using size 8 (5 mm) needles cast on 55 sts and knit 2 rows.

Begin pattern
Row 1: *K1, (k2tog) 3 times, (yf, k1) 5 times, yf, (k2tog) 3 times; rep from * to last st, k1.
Row 2: Knit.
Row 3: Knit.
Row 4: Knit.
Continue working these 4 rows until work measures 12 in (30 cm) ending with a 4th row. Increase 1 at each end of last row and leave 57 sts on a holder.

Second section
Work as for first section, but instead of leaving sts on holder, continue in k3, p3 rib until work measures 68 in (173 cm). Knit one row.

Join the two sections
Graft or bind off together the second section with the sts from the holder from the first section to complete.

YARN REQUIREMENTS
Shetland worsted weight yarn
• Total amount of wool by weight and approximate length:
200 g/476 yds (440 m)

FINISHED SIZES
80 in (203 cm) long

NEEDLES & NOTIONS
One pair size 8 (5 mm) knitting needles

GAUGE
There is no set gauge for this pattern.

Zwartbles fleece

Zwartbles—the name means black with a white blaze—were initially bred to produce milk and meat, and their thick coats were ideal to protect them from the cold, wet, and windy weather. The dense fleece is generally considered as suitable only for making carpets, but enlightened spinners and knitters are starting to use it to create hard-wearing garments.

The fleece of the Zwartbles has virtually no kemp, but it does become slightly tinged with gray when older. The sun bleaches the wool to a reddish brown, so the sheep can appear red in the fields. Because it is so thick, the fleece makes a resilient yarn.

As well as the blaze Zwartbles sheep should have two white socks on the back feet, sometimes also the front feet, and a white tip to the long tail (which is never docked). With their black-and-white markings they are similar to the Balwen Welsh mountain sheep, but the fleece is very different, being denser, consistent, finer, and darker. Any white or silvery fibers are considered undesirable by breeders.

The sheep have bare legs; black, striped, or white feet; large, dark Leicester-style ears; and no horns. They weigh in at 187 lbs (85 kg) for adult ewes and 220 lbs (100 kg) for rams.

In the Netherlands, the breed was recorded as rare by the Dutch Rare Breeds Survival Trust in the 1970s. Recently the easily managed, easy-lambing Zwartbles has seen a revival. In the Netherlands they are still used as milk sheep, particularly for cheese, and work as a complementary enterprise with dairy cattle.

Zwartbles is increasingly popular in the UK, where it was first farmed in the 1990s, as a commercial meat sheep. There are now more than 5,000 Zwartbles in over 200 registered flocks. However, the finer, younger fleeces are not yet seen as worth using for knitting yarns. This is a shame as some of the dark wool is really lovely, and it has a nice resilience.

While a minority in the UK, and not common in the Netherlands, the Zwartbles is no longer rare. No flocks are listed in North America.

BREED AT A GLANCE

Sheep type: European.
Appearance: Black with a white blaze on the nose; no horns.
Rare breeds status: None.
Further information: UK breed society: www.zwartbles.org.
History: Developed in the nineteenth century in Friesland in the Netherlands, when the native Fresian and Drenthe breeds were crossed to create a sheep that would clean-up land that had been grazed by dairy herds.

5-ply Guernsey
worsted yarn

DK yarn

FLEECE FACT FILE
Fleece weight: 4–6.5 lbs (2–3 kg)
Staple length: 4–5 in (10–12.5 cm)
Micron count: 31–34
Crimp: Indistinct
Handle: Crisp
Natural colors: Predominantly black, with some brown
Mixed colors: None
Luster: None

Aran yarn

olive-dyed
Zwartbles/mohair
DK yarn

Close-up of Aran knitted sample

carded fleece

scoured
fleece

raw fleece

Zwartbles yarn

Zwartbles sheep are still relatively new to the knitting wool industry, and yarns made from their fleece are not yet widely used. It is worth some attention as this dark wool has a different texture from dark-colored yarns made from Black Welsh Mountain and Hebridean wool.

Zwartbles fleece that has been bleached red by the sun will come out as a rich bitter chocolate color when spun. A fleece that has been trimmed of any red wool will be a true black.

As with most larger downland sheep, it is well worth getting shearling wool for the best quality. Some Zwartbles wool is very soft and fine, but the average is more like a dark Jacob. We have found that Zwartbles blends beautifully with mohair to create an attractive anthracite silvered black yarn, with the mohair emphasizing the dark of the Zwartbles and taking away the off-black color. This dyes well with olive or purple to make attractive dark yarns.

Dark, crisp, and durable, Zwartbles yarn gives great stitch definition and is best used for outer garments.

The yarn produces dark rugs and tweeds and does not felt easily. The crimp is indistinct and wooly but the yarn is versatile, spinning from 4-ply to Aran. It is more crisp than soft in finish.

We have chosen a cardigan with a textured cable design for our Zwartbles yarn, as it is an ideal wool for outer garments and will last well, maintaining the pattern after wash and wear. Other designs suitable for Zwartbles yarn include the Black Welsh Mountain waistcoat, Galway Aran sweater, Hebridean bag and cushion, Herdwick accessories, North Ronaldsay waistcoat, and Ryeland child's jacket.

Climbing vine cardigan

By Sian Brown

This attractive cardigan has the climbing vine cable, bordered with a neat twisted cable, on either side of the front, mirrored on the back and on each sleeve, all set on a reverse stocking stitch background.

Changing the needle size on the body enables the garment to fit without needing to increase or decrease the number of stitches or adjust the design. The cardigan has a deep welt and wide front bands rising into a wrap collar. It is finished with a single feature button or can be left open as a short stylish jacket.

DESIGNER PROFILE

Sian Brown uses natural wool for most of her designs and loves its tactile feel. She spent the first years of her career designing machine knits for retail suppliers and now designs hand-knits for magazines, yarn companies and book publishers.

YARN REQUIREMENTS

Pure Zwartbles Worsted weight/DK yarn.
U.S. size 8: 450 g/1,071 yds (990 m)
U.S. size 10: 500 g/1,190 yds (1,100 m)
U.S. size 12: 550 g/1,309 yds (1,210 m)
U.S. size 14: 600 g/1,428 yds (1,320 m)
U.S. size 16: 650 g/1,547 yds (1,430 m)
U.S. size 18: 700 g/1,666 yds (1,540 m)

If you wish you can substitute Zwartbles blended with 50% mohair for a softer handle and slight sheen, which enables the cables to be seen even though it is a little more fluffy.

KNITTER PROFILE

Karen Marshalsay was four when her granny taught her to knit, later knitting for shops to supplement her student income. She enjoys traditional knits such as shawls, cables, Fair Isle, ganseys, and socks. She runs www.woolsmithdesigns.com.

Method

Climbing vine and cable panel (worked over 26 sts)
1st row: (WS) P3, k3, p3, k3, p4, C2BP, k5, p3.
2nd row: Sl 1 pw, k2, p4, C2F, k1, T2B, k2, p3, T2F, k1, p3, k2, sl 1pw.
3rd row: Sl 1pw, p2, k3, p2, k4, p2, k1, p3, C2BP, k3, p2, sl 1pw.
4th row: C3L, p3, k3, T2B, p1, k1, C2B, p3, T2F, p3, C3R.
5th row: P3, k7, C2Fp, p2, k2, p4, k3, p3.
6th row: Sl 1 pw, k2, p3, k2, T2B, p2, k1, (C2B) twice, p6, k2, sl 1pw.
7th row: Sl 1pw, p2, k5, C2FP, p4, k3, p3, k3, p2, sl 1pw.
8th row: C3L, p3, k1, T2B, p3, k2, T2F, k1, C2B, p4, C3R.
9th row: P3, k3, C2FP, p3, k1, p2, k4, p2, k3, p3.
10th row: Sl 1 pw, k2, p3, T2B, p3, C2F, k1, p1, T2F, k3, p3, k2, sl 1pw.
11th row: Sl 1pw, p2, k3, p4, k2, p2, C2Bp, k7, p2, sl 1pw.
12th row: C3L, p6, (C2F) twice, k1, p2, T2F, k2, p3, C3R.
These 12 rows form the pattern.

MEASUREMENTS
Bust size: 30-32 (34-36, 38-40, 42-44, 46-48, 50-52) in (77-82 (87-92, 107-112, 117-122, 127-132) cm)
Garment size: 35.5 (39.75, 44, 48.5, 52.75, 57) in (90 (101, 112, 123, 134, 145) cm)
Length: 19.75 (20.5, 21.25, 22, 22.75, 23.5) in (50 (52, 54, 56, 58, 60) cm)
Instructions are given for the smallest size first, followed by the larger sizes in brackets.

SKILL LEVEL 🧶🧶

NEEDLES & NOTIONS
One pair each of needles size 4 (3.25 mm), size 5 (3.75 mm) and size 6 (4 mm).
Cable needle
One large button or toggle to fasten

GAUGE
Approx 22 sts x 28 rows = 4 in (10 cm) over st st on size 6 (4 mm) needles
Adjust needle size to give required tension

ABBREVIATIONS (see also page 140)
C2PB (cross 2 back purl-wise): slip next st onto a cable needle and hold at back of work, p1, then p1 from cable needle.
C2PF (cross 2 front purl-wise): slip next st onto a cable needle and hold at front of work, p1, then p1 from cable needle.
C2B (cross 2 back, knit-wise): slip next st onto a cable needle and hold at back of work, k1, then k1 from cable needle.
C2F (cross 2 front, knit-wise): slip next st onto a cable needle and hold at front of work, k1, then k1 from cable needle.
T2B (twist 2 back): slip next st onto a cable needle and hold at back of work, k1, then p1 from cable needle.
T2F (twist 2 front): slip next st onto a cable needle and hold at front of work, p1, then k1 from cable needle.
C3L (cable 3 left): slip next st onto a cable needle and hold at front of work, k2, then k1 from cable needle.
C3R (cable 3 right): slip next 2 sts onto a cable needle and hold at back of work, k1, then k2 from cable needle.

BACK (make 1)
Using size 5 (3.75 mm) needles cast on 106 (118, 130, 142, 154, 166) sts.
1st row: P2, (k2, p2) to end.
2nd row: K2, (p2, k2) to end.
These 2 rows form the rib.
Work a further 15 rows.

Change to size 6 (4 mm) needles.
1st row: (WS) K14 (18, 22, 26, 30, 34), work across 1st row of pattern panel, k26 (30, 34, 38, 42, 46) work across 1st row of pattern panel, k14 (18, 22, 26, 30, 34).
2nd row: P14 (18, 22, 26, 30, 34), work across 2nd row of pattern panel, p 26 (30, 34, 38, 42, 46) work across 2nd row of pattern panel, p 14 (18, 22, 26, 30, 34).
These 2 rows set cable panel with reversed st st between.

Continue in pattern until back measures 3 (3, 3½, 3½) in (7 (7, 8, 8, 9, 9) cm) from cast on edge, ending with a wrong side row.
Change back to 3.75 mm (US 5) needles to shapw waist. Work 18 rows. Change back to 4 mm (US 6) needles. Continue in pattern until back measures 11¾ (12¼, 12½, 13, 13¼, 13½) in (30 (31, 32, 33, 34, 35) cm) from cast on edge, ending with a wrong side row.

Shape armholes
Bind off 5 (6, 7, 8, 9, 10) sts at beginning of next 2 rows. 96 (106, 116, 126, 136, 146) sts. Decrease one st at each end of the next and 7 (8, 9, 10, 11, 12) following alternate rows. 80 (88, 96, 104, 112, 120) sts. Continue in pattern until back measures 19¾ (20½, 21¼, 22, 22¾, 23½) in (50 (52, 54, 56, 58, 60) cm) from cast on edge, ending with a wrong side row.

Shape shoulders
Bind off 8 (9, 10, 11, 12, 13) sts at beginning of next 6 rows. Bind off remaining 32 (34, 36, 38, 40, 42) sts.

LEFT FRONT
(make 1)
Using 3.75 mm (US 5) needles cast on 49 (53, 61, 65, 73, 77) sts.
1st row: P2, (k2, p2) to last 3 sts, k3.
2nd row: P3, k2, (p2, k2) to end
Work a further 15 rows.

Change to 4 mm (US 6) needles.
1st row: (WS) K9 (9, 13, 13, 17, 17) work across 1st row of patt panel, k14 (18, 22, 26, 30, 34)
2nd row: P 14 (18, 22, 26, 30, 34), work across 2nd row of patt panel, p9 (9, 13, 13, 17, 17) These rows set the cable panel with reversed st st between. Continue in pattern until front measures 3 (3, 3½, 3½) in

35½ (39¾, 44, 48½, 52¾, 57) in
90 (101, 112, 123, 134, 145) cm

11¾, 12½, 13, 13¼, 13½) in
30 (31, 32, 33, 34, 35) cm

19¾ (20½, 22, 22¾, 23½) in
(50 (52, 54 56, 58, 60) cm)

SLEEVE

18 (18, 18½, 19, 19) in
46 (46, 47, 47, 48, 48) cm

(7 (7, 8, 8, 9, 9) cm) from cast on edge, ending with wrong side row.

Change to 3.75 mm (US 5) needles. Work a further 18 rows.

Change back to 4 mm (US 6) needles. Continue in pattern until 12 rows less have been worked than on back to armhole shaping, ending with a wrong side row.

Shape neck
Next row: pattern to last 2 sts, work 2 tog.
Work 3 rows.
Rep the last 4 rows 3 times more. 45 (49, 57, 61, 69, 73) sts.
Shape armhole
Next row: Bind off 5 (6, 7, 8, 9, 10) sts, pattern to last 2 sts work 2 tog. 39 (42, 49, 52, 59, 62) sts. Work 1 row.
Continue to decrease at neck edge on every 4th row **at the same time** decrease one st at armhole edge of the next and 7 (8, 9, 10, 11, 12) following alternate rows.
Keeping armhole edge straight continue to decrease at neck edge on every 4th row until

24 (27, 30, 33, 36, 39) sts remain. Work straight until front measures same as back to shoulder, ending at armhole edge.

Shape shoulder
Bind off 8 (9, 10, 11, 12, 13) sts at beginningof next and following alternate row.
Work 1 row. Bind off remaining 8(9, 10, 11, 12, 13) sts.

RIGHT FRONT (make 1)
Using size 5 (3.75 mm) needles cast on 49 (53, 61, 65, 73, 77) sts.
1st row: K3, p2, (k2, p2) to end.
2nd row: K2, (p2, k2) to last 3 sts, p3.
Work a further 15 rows in rib.
Change to size 6 (4 mm) needles.
1st row: (WS) K14 (18, 22, 26, 30, 34) work across 1st row of patt panel, k9 (9, 13, 13, 17, 17).
2nd row: P9 (9, 13, 13, 17, 17), work across 2nd row of patt panel, p14 (18, 22, 26, 30, 34). These 2 rows set the cable panel with reversed st st between.
Continue in pattern until front measures 3 (3, 3½, 3½) in (7 (7, 8,

8, 9, 9) cm) from cast on edge, ending with a wrong side row. Change to size 5 (3.75 mm) needles. Work a further 18 rows. Change to size 6 (4 mm) needles. Continue in pattern until 12 rows fewer have been worked than on back to armhole shaping, ending with a wrong side row.

Shape neck
Next row: Work 2tog, pattern to end. Work 3 rows.
Rep the last 4 rows 3 times more.
Next row: Work 2tog, pattern to end, leaving 44 (48, 56, 60, 68, 72) sts.

Shape armhole
Next row Bind off 5(6, 7, 8, 9, 10) sts, pattern to end. 39 (42, 49, 52, 59, 62) sts.
Continue to decrease at neck edge on every 4th row **and at the same time** decrease 1st at armhole edge of the next and 7 (8, 9, 10, 11, 12) following alternate rows.
Keeping armhole edge straight continue to decrease at neck edge on every 4th row until 24 (27, 30, 33, 36, 39) sts remain. Work straight until front measures the same as back to shoulder, ending at armhole edge.

Shape shoulder
Bind off 8 (9, 10, 11, 12, 13) sts at beginning of next and following alternate row.
Work 1 row.
Bind off remaining 8 (9, 10, 11, 12, 13) sts.

SLEEVES (make 2)
Using size 3 (3.25 mm) needles cast on 38 (42, 46, 50, 54, 58) sts.

1st, 3rd and 5th sizes only
1st row: P2, (k2, p2) to end.
2nd row: K2, (p2, k2) to end.

2nd, 4th and 6th sizes only
1st row: K2, (p2, k2) to end.
2nd row: P2, (k2, p2) to end.

All sizes
These 2 rows form the rib. Work a further 15 rows. Change to size 6 (4 mm) needles.
1st row: (WS) K6 (8, 10, 12, 14, 16), work across 1st row of patt panel, k6 (8, 10, 12, 14, 16).
2nd row: P6 (8, 10, 12, 14, 16), work across 2nd row of patt panel, p6 (8, 10, 12, 14, 16).

These 2 rows set the cable panel with reversed st st between. Work 5 rows.
Increase row P3, m1, patt to last 3 sts, m1, p3.
Repeat the last 6 rows 17 times more. 74 (78, 82, 86, 90, 94) sts.

Continue straight until sleeve measures 18 (18, 18½, 18½, 19, 19) in (46 (46, 47, 47, 48, 48) cm) from cast on edge, ending with wrong side row.

Shape top
Bind off 5 (6, 7, 8, 9, 10) sts at beginning of next 2 rows. 64 (66, 68, 70, 72, 74) sts.
Work 0 (2, 0, 2, 0, 2) rows.
1st row: pattern to end.
2nd row: pattern to end.
3rd row: Work 2 tog, pattern to last 2sts, work 2tog.
4th row: pattern to end.
Repeat the last 4 rows 3 (3, 4, 4, 5, 5) times more, to make 56 (58, 58, 60, 60, 62) sts.
Bind off 4 sts at beginning of next 12 rows, leaving 8 (10, 10, 12, 12, 14) sts. Bind off .

LEFT FRONT BAND and COLLAR (make 1)
Using size 3 (3.25 mm) needles, and with right side facing, cast on 22 (22, 26, 26, 30, 30) sts, pick up and k 54 (56, 58, 60, 62, 64) sts to beginning of neck shaping, 58 (60, 62, 64, 66, 68) sts to cast on edge. 134 (138, 146, 150, 158, 162) sts in total.
1st row: P2, (k2, p2) to end.
This row sets the rib.
Next 2 rows: Rib 22 (22, 26, 26, 30, 30) turn, rib to end.

Next 2 rows: Rib 26 (26, 30, 30, 34, 34) turn, rib to end.
Next 2 rows: Rib 30 (30, 34, 34, 38, 38) turn, rib to end.
Next 2 rows: Rib 34 (34, 38, 38, 42, 42) turn, rib to end.
Next 2 rows: Rib 38 (38, 42, 42, 46, 46) turn, rib to end.
Continue in this way working 4 extra sts on every alternate row until row rib 74 (74, 82, 82, 90, 90) turn, rib to end, has been worked.
Rib 12 (12, 12, 14, 14, 14) rows across all sts. Bind off in rib.

RIGHT FRONT BAND (make 1)
Using size 3 (3.25 mm) needles, and with RS facing, pick up and k 58 (60, 62, 64, 66, 68) sts to beginning of neck shaping, 54 (56, 58, 60, 62, 64) sts to shoulder seam, cast on 22 (22, 26, 26, 30, 30) sts, to make a total of 134 (138, 146, 150, 158, 162) sts.
Work in p2, k2 rib as follows:
Next 2 rows: Rib 22 (22, 26, 26, 30, 30) turn, rib to end.
Next 2 rows: Rib 26 (26, 30, 30, 34, 34) turn, rib to end.
Next 2 rows: Rib 30 (30, 34, 34, 38, 38) turn, rib to end.
Next 2 rows: Rib 34 (34, 38, 38, 42, 42) turn, rib to end.
Next 2 rows: Rib 38 (38, 42, 42, 46, 46) turn, rib to end.
Continue in this way working 4 extra sts on every alternate row until the row rib 74 (74, 82, 82, 90, 90) turn, rib to end, has been worked. Rib 5 rows across all sts.
1st buttonhole row: Rib 50 (52, 54, 56, 58, 60), bind off 3 sts, rib to end.
2nd buttonhole row: Rib, casting on 3 sts over those bind off.
Work 5 (5, 5, 7, 7, 7) rows across all sts. Bind off in rib.

MAKE UP
Join collar row ends. Sew collar to back neck. Join side and sleeve seams. Sew in sleeves. Sew on button.

pure wool
practicals

Yarn selector

What makes a good quality knitting yarn? Generally, we want finer and softer fleeces as these are more comfortable. However, do not ignore the character of the wool—it is unreasonable to expect even the very finest Hebridean to be as fine as the finest Shetland, so this must also be taken into account.

A healthy sheep will produce better wool, irrespective of all other factors, so this is the most important starting point. Sheep who are well cared for, living in an environment appropriate for their breed and age, will produce good wool. Then many more specific factors that relate to the individual sheep come in to play.

Breed

Genetics affects wool in two ways: the genes of the breed (Black Welsh Mountain is very different from Cotswold, for example), and the genes of an individual animal (some Black Welsh Mountain sheep have coarser, or darker, or crimpier fleeces than others within a flock).

These factors become even more pronounced with mules and other cross-bred sheep, and are also characteristic of primitive sheep: for example North Ronaldsay, Gotland, and Shetland are more varied in color and fleece style than other sheep.

Generally, darker colored wools are coarser and paler,

Wool Characteristics and Yarn Types

BREED	Rarity	Staple length	Fleece weight	Micron	Luster	Fiber type
BLACK WELSH MOUNTAIN	recovering	3–4 in (6–10 cm)	3–4 lbs (1.25–2 kg)	32–35	no	medium
BLUE-FACED LEICESTER	not rare	3–6 in (6–15 cm)	2–4 lbs (1–2 kg)	26–26.5	semi	fine
CASTLEMILK MOORIT	vulnerable	2–3 in (5–8 cm)	2.2 lbs (1 kg)	30–31.5	no	fine
CORRIEDALE/FALKLANDS	not rare	3–5 in (7.5–12.5 cm)	10–13 lbs (4.5–6 kg)	26–33	no	fine
COTSWOLD	threatened	7–12 in (17.5–30 cm)	9–15 lbs (4–7 kg)	34–40	yes	medium
GALWAY	conservation	4.5–7.5 in (11–19 cm)	5.5–7.7lbs (2.5–3.5 kg)	30	semi	medium
GOTLAND	rare in UK	3–5 in (8–12 cm)	2–8 lbs (1–4 kg)	28–32	yes	medium
HEBRIDEAN	native to UK	2–6 in (5–15 cm)	2–4 lbs (1–2 kg)	35+	some	strong
HERDWICK	vulnerable	2–4 in (10–20 cm)	2–4 lbs (1.5–2 kg)	35+	no	strong
JACOB	threatened	3–6 in (8–15 cm)	3–5 lbs (1.75–2.75 kg)	28–35	no	medium
MANX LOAGTHAN	conservation	2.5–4 in (7–10 cm)	2–4 lbs (1–2 kg)	30	no	medium
NORTH RONALDSAY	endangered	1.5–3 in (4–8 cm)	2–4 lbs (1–2 kg)	25–40	no	medium
ROMNEY	not rare	4–7 in (10–17 cm)	7–11 lbs (3–5 kg)	30–34	yes	medium
RYELAND	native to UK	3–4 in (7.5–10 cm)	4–5 lbs (2–2.75 kg)	28–32	no	medium
SHETLAND	native to UK	2–4 in (5–10 cm)	2.2 lbs (1 kg)	12–30	no	fine
ZWARTBLES	not rare	4–5 in (10–12.5 cm)	4–6.5lbs (2–3 kg)	31–34	no	medium

and colored wools are finer, across and within breeds and, in the case of Jacob sheep, sometimes even on the same sheep!

Rams usually have coarser coats than ewes, and wethers tend to keep lamb characteristics, so their fleeces are more like those of ewes than rams.

Age

Young sheep have finer fleeces, with lambs and shearlings being the best. As sheep get older they produce coarser fleeces. However, some older sheep have fine fleeces because of their genetics, and it is by no means a rule that a lamb will have finer wool than a ewe of the same breed.

The fleeces of each breed are very different to look at and feel—and remember that feeling the soft wool on a sheep's back, or just after shearing, is feeling it at its best. Once we process and twist the wool into yarns it becomes harder. This is why a soft, fine wool such as Gotland may not feel as soft when in a ball but, with washing and wearing, will gradually soften.

Wools that tend to felt will soften more with age than

The table below summarizes the characteristics of the breeds we have covered in this book, and shows the most appropriate yarns we think they will make. It includes whether woolen or worsted yarns are preferable, whether blending is useful, and what fibers can be usefully blended with the basic wool of particular breeds. Where a wool is either very rare or pretty good as it is, we have suggested leaving well alone! But some that are nice, but less rare, are worth experimenting with to get more variety, while others benefit by becoming softer or better by blending. Adding mohair to darker wools increases softness and produces a better result from dyeing. Adding a small amount of colored wool to a white wool adds interest and a more subtle effect with dyeing.

Handle	Lace	4-ply Sportweight	DK Worsted	Aran Medium	Chunky Bulky	Gurnsey	Other possible yarns	Better Worsted	Better Woolen	Good Blended	Purpose of blend	Blend suggestions
soft			•	•	•		4-ply	no	yes	yes		
soft		•	•				aran, chunky	either	either	possible	variety	silk, flax
medium			•	•			chunky		yes	yes	improve	silk, alpaca
soft		•	•	•	•			either	either	possible	variety	silk, flax, Manx Loagthan, Hebridean, Black Welsh Mountain
medium			•	•			4-ply, chunky	yes	no	no		
medium				•	•	•	DK	either	either	no		
soft		•	•	•			lace, chunky	no	yes	possible	variety	silk, Merino, Corriedale
strong			•	•	•		4-ply	no	yes	yes	improve	Manx Loagthan, mohair
strong				•	•		DK	no	yes	yes	improve	mohair
medium			•	•	•	•	4-ply	either	either	yes	variety	mohair, alpaca
medium			•				chunky, guernsey	no	yes	yes	improve	Hebridean, mohair
medium			•	•	•			no	yes	no		
medium			•	•		•	chunky	either	either	possible	variety	Manx Loagthan, Hebridean
medium			•	•	•		4-ply	no	yes	yes	variety	colored Ryeland
soft	•	•	•				aran	no	yes	yes	variety	colored Shetland
medium			•	•	•	•	4-ply	no	yes	yes	improve	mohair, alpaca

those that are less easy to felt, and worsted-spun yarns will felt less than woolen-spun yarns. Similarly, a luster yarn will produce a different appearance, and feel smoother, even if coarser, than a non-luster yarn.

Some yarns, though, are naturally very soft, these include Corriedale and Shetland, even though they have no luster.

But this is only the beginning, as yarns from each breed have individual characteristics. As the *Wool Qualities and Yarn Types* chart (below) shows, soft wools do not necessarily make fine or drapey yarns, and coarse wools do not inevitably have to be consigned to the Aran section. Also a luster wool will be considerably denser than a non-luster, so will make very heavy garments if used as a worsted-spun yarn, in chunky weight, or for larger items. In fact, it is better to use woolen-spun, semi-luster, or non-luster yarns for these.

The patterns in this book have been designed with a view to the most suitable projects. If you have a similar pattern it will probably work in the yarn we have chosen. For example, many accessories such as scarves and mittens, as well as cushions, will work in plenty of different yarns from several breeds.

Wool Qualities and Yarn Types

BREED	Micron	Luster	Fiber type	Handle	Lace	4-ply Sportweight	DK Worsted	Aran Medium	Chunky Bulky	Gurnsey
HERDWICK	35+	no	strong	strong			■	■	■	
HEBRIDEAN	35+	some	strong	strong		░	■	■	■	
COTSWOLD	34–40	yes	medium	medium			■	■	░	
BLACK WELSH MOUNTAIN	32–35	no	medium	soft		░	■	■	■	
NORTH RONALDSAY	25–40	no	medium	medium			■	■	■	
ZWARTBLES	31–34	no	medium	medium			■	■	■	
GALWAY	30+	semi	medium	medium			■	░		■
MANX LOAGHTAN	30+	no	medium	medium			■	■	░	░
ROMNEY	30–34	yes	medium	medium			■	■		■
CASTLEMILK MOORIT	30–31.5	no	fine	medium		░	■	■	░	
RYELAND	28–32	no	medium	medium		░	■	■	■	
JACOB	28–35	no	medium	medium			■	■	■	■
GOTLAND	28–32	yes	medium	soft		░	■	■		
CORRIEDALE/FALKLANDS	26–33	no	fine	soft		■	■	■	■	
BLUE-FACED LEICESTER	26–26.5	semi	fine	soft		■	■	■		
SHETLAND	12–30	no	fine	soft	■	■	■	■		

The chart above lists the wools in order of the micron count rather than alphabetically, so that the gradual change in suitability of yarns from fine to thicker can be seen more clearly.

■ The dark shading shows the first choice of appropriate yarns for the particular wool.

░ The pale shading gives possible options, either with the help of a bit of alpaca or mohair, or by choosing finer fleeces.

Substitutions

If you choose a different breed of sheep for a project, bear in mind the appropriate yarn ranges shown in *Wool Qualities and Yarn Types* (see page 134). For example, it will not work as well to make an Aran pattern in a yarn such as Blue-faced Leicester or Shetland, or to make a 4-ply pattern from a yarn such as Manx Loagthan or Romney (unless they have been blended with a fiber to help the yarn work better). However, if you choose a project such as the Scallop Shell Top (see page 28), which needs luster and definition, and want an alternative to Blue-faced Leicester (it is nice in an alpaca yarn, by the way), it will not work as well in Corriedale, which has no luster, or in Gotland, which felts with wear.

Some of the designs in the book are very specific to the breed of sheep and the wool it produces. The most obvious case is the Shetland Fair Isle waistcoat (see page 118), although this could, at a push, be done with natural and dyed Jacob (not so soft though) or with North Ronaldsay (a different shading and texture so less distinct, which would make the design fuzzy).

Better Worsted	Better Woolen	Good for	Bad for	Key characteristics in yarn
no	yes	accessories	next to skin	Coarse, kempy but great heathered colors
no	yes	accessories	next to skin	A good dark off-black, strong, lambs can be very soft, slight luster in lambs
yes	no	near skin	detail/cable	Strong, lustrous, and creamy with ideal long staple for worsted, lambs fine
no	yes	near skin	detail/cable	Soft and a good dark almost black, versatile
no	yes	outerwear	detail/cable	Double coat, fine and coarse, feels reasonably soft, good natural color range
either	yes	outerwear	detail/cable	Nice bouncy, off-black, good general option between Hebridean and Black Welsh Mountain
no	either	near skin		Good general purpose medium, semi-luster yarn, some dark hairs add interest
either	yes	outerwear		Brown, bouncy, short, bulky, if long enough can be worsted-spun
no	either	near skin		Nice creamy yarn, long enough for worsted, good mixed and all-rounder
no	yes	near skin	hard wear	Rare, short, and needs a bit of help, but OK for pure blends in thicker yarns
either	yes	outerwear		Nice bouncy, reasonably soft wool, two good colors to mix and match
maybe	either	near skin		Very versatile in color range, good work-horse alone and blends and dyes well
either	yes	near skin	detail/cable	True gray, luster, long, can pill and shed in worsted due to smooth fibers working out, dyes beautifully
either	either	next to skin	hard wear	Very white, soft, bulky, versatile, dyes well, will blend well to add interest
no	either	next to skin	outerwear	Lovely creamy, soft semi-luster, can feel a bit spongy when soft worsted-spun
no	yes	next to skin	accessories	Every natural color, soft and very fine, will blend with alpaca for smoothness and brighter natural colors

• Corriedale and Blue-faced Leicester are both soft and fine, but the first is bulky and the second is lean so use Corriedale for warmth and Blue-faced Leicester for drape.

• The long luster wools do not make good chunky yarns as they are dense, so the yarns become heavy if made thick—this is also the case with alpaca.

• Wensleydale would be better than Cotswold for 4-ply and lace-weight and is similar in style.

• North Ronaldsay makes a soft 4-ply if de-haired of its coarse hairs but loses its character—better to use Shetland.

• Near skin means people able to wear wool should be able to wear this next to skin, but others will need something between them and the wool!

• **For bulk and warmth use:** Black Welsh Mountain, North Ronaldsay, Manx Loagthan, Ryeland, Corriedale/Falkland, Shetland.

• **For drape and sheen use:** Cotswold, Gotland, Blue-faced Leicester.

• **For intermediate or individual use:** Herdwick, Hebridean, Zwartbles, Galway, Romney, Castlemilk Moorit, Jacob.

It is a relatively safe bet to use a Jacob yarn for most knitting patterns, and the designs for Jacob yarns included in this book will work in many different breed yarns because Jacob is such a versatile wool. In fact, once you blend Jacob with mohair—and if you dye it as well—you could probably spend the rest of your life without knitting with another breed, unless you want to make lace!

Gauge

This is all useful, **BUT it is vitally important to remember that if you need the measurements of your work to be exact you MUST make a gauge swatch—the bigger the better—as it will also illustrate the drape and handle of the resulting fabric.** If you just pin it out very slightly stretched on a cushion to count the stitches and rows, and do not wash and press it, it will be sufficiently accurate, and you just rip it back to use in your main project.

It is a relatively complex exercise to grade a pattern made for a 4-ply yarn for a Double Knitting or thicker yarn, and vice-versa, so it is much better to get the correct yarn weight for your project. A useful rule of thumb is that, with Blacker Yarns (but not all yarns!),

Matching yarns to patterns

Remember you will need to change the yarn or re-scale the pattern if you try some of the other options

Breed	Main pattern	Yarn UK name	Cozy body-warmer	Scallop shell top	Baby's log cabin blanket	Cable and rib sweater	Hot-water bottle cover	Wavy cable jumper	Pucker cable
BLACK WELSH MOUNTAIN	Cozy body-warmer	DK	■						
BLUE-FACED LEICESTER	Scallop shell top	DK		■					
BLUE-FACED LEICESTER	Baby's log cabin blanket	DK			■				
CASTLEMILK MOORIT	Cable and rib sweater	DK				■			
CORRIEDALE/FALKLANDS	Hot-water bottle cover	2 x DK					■		
COTSWOLD	Wavy cable jumper	DK						■	
GALWAY	Pucker cable tunic	Aran							
GOTLAND	Ladies cardigan with pockets	DK							
GOTLAND	Fall leaves beret	4-ply							
HEBRIDEAN	Hebridean handbag	2 x Aran							
HEBRIDEAN	Sanquhar cushion	DK							
HERDWICK	Tea, cafetière and egg cosies	Aran							
JACOB	Jacob cable jacket	2 x DK							
JACOB/MOHAIR*	Socks for walking and rain boots	4 x and Aran							
MANX LOAGHTAN	Zig-zag scarf, hat and mittens	DK							
NORTH RONALDSAY	Airy waistcoat	Aran							
ROMNEY	Traditional Guernsey pullover	Guernsey							
RYELAND	Ryeland child's hooded jacket	2 x DK							
SHETLAND	Shetland spot waistcoat	4-ply							
SHETLAND	Shetland feather and fan scarf	DK							
ZWARTBLES	Climbing vine cardigan	DK							

SUMMARY FOR BREED SPECIFIC YARNS

Breed yarn for pattern

Breed yarns possible for pattern

Breed yarns borderline for pattern

Breed yarns not recommended for pattern

* for Jacob/mohair, other blends with mohair such as Manx, Hebridean and Zwartbles would also be appropriate two strands of 4-ply are equivalent to Aran and two strands of Double Knitting are equivalent to Chunky.

Needle size

You can enlarge a design simply by knitting it in a thicker yarn on larger needles, or reduce it by using a thinner yarn and smaller needles. Again you should make a gauge swatch to work out how much larger or smaller your project will be. Once you know how many stitches make up 4 in or 10 cm, you can work out from the pattern (use the back or the maximum number of stitches if in the round) how many inches or centimeters you will create by casting on the stitches specified for each size. Therefore you will know how much larger or smaller your own project will be.

Care advice

Hand-wash pure wool in cool water using a liquid wool wash. You can spin the knitted garment but do not tumble dry. Instead, spread on a towel, hand-pressing it into shape and to the correct size and leave to dry. Store folded. If a garment requires ironing, press on the wrong side when almost dry. Do not iron ribbing.

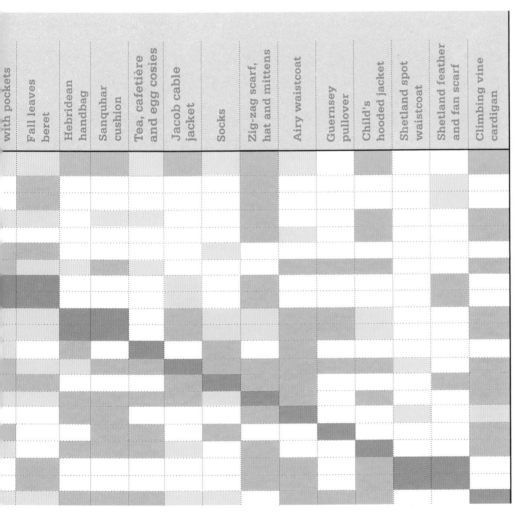

The chart left shows the patterns we have designed as most appropriate for each yarn in the darkest shade, with a range of paler and palest shades. You should obtain a satisfactory result in the paler shade, but may be taking wool and yarn too far from its natural preference in the palest shades. We have used UK yarn names, as these are the recommended yarns; U.S. equivalents are shown on *Wool Qualities and Yarn Types* (see page 134) and *Yarn Terminology* (page 16).

Dyeing pure wool

Weaving and crochet are beyond the scope of this book, but here is a small introduction to dyeing. Dyeing is like cookery— it can be very creative and satisfying, but as you are dealing with natural materials it can also be variable!

Wool (such as mohair, silk, and alpaca) is a fiber made of protein, so it will dye differently to cotton, hemp, or flax, which are vegetable, or artificial fibers, which are mineral. However, different wool fibers will dye differently, so it is possible to put, say, Galway, Romney, and White Ryeland into the same dye at the same time, and they will all come out slightly differently (if blue, of course they will all be blue, but the blues will differ!).

We recommend only dyeing some of your yarn and using it with the natural colors to enhance them— many of the patterns in this book work well with a welt and cuffs in a darker or brighter color, or with stripes.

If you are intending to use only dyed yarn, take note of the comments in *Wool Qualities and Yarn Types* (see page 134) and remember that dyeing colored yarn will leave the natural color as the base and not white!

If you wish to mix dyed and naturally colored yarns in a project, avoid primary colors as these can clash. However, red and yellow work with dark natural wools, and blue works with white or brown (when it will seem gray). To achieve these contrasts, dye white wool.

Key points:
• Dye wool in LOOSELY tied hanks: if tied tightly the dye cannot reach all of the wool and it will be patchy.

Wool Colors and Dye Ideas

BREED	MAIN COLOR	Off-black	Dark brown	Brown gray	Mid-brown	Fawn	Creamy white	Ivory white	White	Pale gray	Mid-gray	Dark gray
		■	■	■	■	■	■		□	■	■	■
BLACK WELSH MOUNTAIN	black	■	■	■								
BLUE-FACED LEICESTER	creamy white						■					
CASTLEMILK MOORIT	mid-brown				■							
CORRIEDALE/FALKLANDS	very white								□			
COTSWOLD	creamy white						■					
GALWAY	ivory white											
GOTLAND	gray									■	■	■
HEBRIDEAN	black	■	■	■								
HERDWICK	multi					■			□		■	■
JACOB	mid-gray	■	■	■					□			
MANX LOAGTHAN	mid-brown				■							
NORTH RONALDSAY	multi		■							■	■	■
ROMNEY	milk white											
RYELAND	multi					■						■
SHETLAND	multi	■	■	■	■	■	■		□	■	■	■
ZWARTBLES	black	■	■						□			

- Wash the wool well beforehand: any residual grease will make the result patchy.
- The wool must be evenly and completely wetted without trapped air: otherwise it will be patchy.
- Bring the wool and dye to boiling point to activate the chemicals. DO NOT agitate it as this could cause felting.
- Different dyes work at different temperatures, so it is very important to raise the temperature SLOWLY or again there is risk of patchiness or color variation.
- If you want to repeat a color, you must measure and work accurately and write down what you do, keeping a sample of each dye-lot.
- Glass, enamel, or stainless steel utensils work best—aluminum, copper, and iron may react with the dyes.
- Cover yourself, your floor, and your work surfaces to protect them from the dye.
- Some dyestuffs are poisonous, so you should wear gloves, protective glasses, and a face mask when dealing with very fine powders in particular.
- Dyes need auxiliary chemicals to help them work, usually to neutralize or acidify the water—most wool dyes require acid conditions to fix them and the dye bonds chemically with the fiber, so your dye-bath should be almost colorless when you have finished (if it is not, you can re-use it to dye something a paler color).

A simple dye to try is the drink Kool Aid (we wonder what color our insides become if we drink it). Also cold tea works well for a brown, but these are effectively dyeing by staining rather than by chemicals.

Many vegetable dyes vary from batch to batch so it is worth a trial first. Some of these fade fast in daylight—although strong sunlight will bleach everything, including dark naturally colored wools (which is why they are usually off-black). There are many excellent books on dyeing and growing plants to make dyes, so even if you are unable to grow your own wool you can add a little home-grown personality to your yarns.

DYE IDEAS	NOTES AND SUGGESTIONS
no	could dye blue, purple, or red to alter off-black
any pastel	remember the golden base will affect the dyed result!
red, gold, brown	the brown can be a bit dull, but it's rare, so better natural
any bright	can look a bit artificial when dyed, unless blended
any pastel or bright	good for dyeing due to luster, but cream base will affect dyed result a bit
any pastel	as this is rare, I would probably leave it natural
blue, wine, purple, olive, gold	lovely heathered shades when dyed, with great depth
no	could dye blue, purple, or red to alter off-black
blue, wine, purple, olive, gold	lovely heathered shades when dyed, with great depth
blue, wine, purple, olive, gold	a good base for experimenting with plain and heathered shades
red, gold, brown	better to blend with mohair and then dye, probably
blue, wine, purple, olive, gold	rare and nice as it is, would not bother to dye!
any pastel	some natural and some with, say, olive or denim blue, for two-color designs
blue, wine, purple, olive, gold	the colored is very nice undyed, so probably better to use Jacob!
no	lovely as it is, would not bother to dye!
no	could dye blue, purple, or red to alter off-black

Knitting know-how

On the following pages you will find information about the abbreviations and technical terms used in the patterns in this book, plus advice on making-up and caring for your pure wool knitwear.

Abbreviations

Alt: alternate.
Dec (Decrease): Knit or purl 2 stitches together, or s1, k1, psso on knit rows and p2togtbl on purl rows.
DPN: Double Pointed Needles.
Inc (Increase): Knit or purl into both the front and back of a st, to create 2 stitches.
k: knit.
K2tog or P2tog: knit or purl the next 2 stitches together.
k2togtbl: knit two stitches together through the back of the loop (rather than the front).
K3tog or P3tog: knit or purl the next 3 stitches together.
K tbl: through back loop.
Kw: knitwise.
m1(make one): pick up loop between st just worked and next st and knit into back of loop.
p: purl.
p2togtbl: purl two stitches together through the back of the loop (rather than the front).
psso: pass the slipped st over the next knitted st.
Pw: purlwise.
RS: right side.
sl: slip a st from one needle to the other.

st. st: stocking stitch.
st, sts: stitch, stitches.
SM: stitch marker.
Tog: together.
Tw2: twist 2 stitches—take the needle past the first st knit into second st, then knit first st, slip both stitches off the needle together.
WS: wrong side.
yf: (yarn forward, sometimes called "yarn over"). Pass the yarn over the needle between two stitches, making a loop, which you knit or purl into in the next row to create an extra st.

Stitches

Garter stitch: knit every row.
Stocking stitch: Row 1 (RS): knit to end; Row 2 (WS): purl to end; repeat these 2 rows.
Reverse stocking stitch: Row 1 (RS): purl to end; Row 2 (WS): knit to end; repeat these 2 rows.
Moss stitch: alternate rows of k1, p1, so the knit stitches are over the purl stitches on the previous row.
Seed stitch: another name for moss stitch.
2 x 2 rib: Row 1: (k2, p2) repeat to end. Row 2: (p2, k2) repeat to end. Repeat these rows for the required number of rows or the required length is reached.

English, Continental, or long-tail cast-on: Unwind 1 in (2.5 cm) yarn for each st, plus a tail. Make a slip knot at this point in the yarn and place it on needle in your right hand. Hold length of yarn in your left hand. Pass it around your left thumb and hold in against the palm of your hand with your fourth and fifth fingers. Insert point of needle into loop around your thumb. Bring yarn from ball around needle and draw it through loop around your thumb to create a st on the needle, slipping loop off your thumb as you do so. Tighten st on needle and make a new loop around your thumb ready for next st.
Cable cast-on: Make a slip knot and place it on the needle in your left hand. With the yarn and second needle in your right hand, insert tip of right-hand needle into the loop on the left-hand needle and pass the yarn around the tip. Use the tip to pull the yarn through and place the loop you have created onto the left-hand needle to make second st. To make the third, and all subsequent stitches, insert the tip of the right-hand needle between the first and second stitches and knit a st between them.

Magic loop

This method allows you to knit in the round using one long circular needle instead of a set of DPNs. Cast on and slide stitches onto the cable. Find the center of the row and pull the cable through at this point to make a large loop. Arrange stitches so half are on each needle. Both needles should point in the same direction and the last stitches worked should be at the rear. Move rear-needle stitches to cable and knit stitches on front needle. There will be a loop of cable at both sides of work. When you have worked all stitches on front needle (half the round), slip rear-needle stitches back onto needle and turn your work. Repeat steps 3 and 4 as required.

Making-up tips

Blocking: Darn in all ends and then wash all pieces. Gently squeeze out excess water and then, on a flat surface padded with towels, pin out the pieces to the dimensions given in the pattern and leave until dry. Alternatively, pin out the dry, unwashed knitting and spray with water, then leave to dry. Or, press on the wrong side using a steam iron (pad the ironing board with a towel).
Joning seams: generally a simple backstitch is ideal for this. However, for a "hidden" seam, use **Mattress stitch**: place both pieces on a flat surface, side-by-side and with right sides facing. Attach yarn to right-hand side and bring needle to front between first and second stitches of first row. Take thread under loop between first and second stitches of first row on left-hand side of seam. Repeat on right-hand side. Continue to complete seam.

Finishing sock toes:
Kitchener stitch creates an invisible seam at the toe of a sock. Using a large needle and spare yarn, or the tail from the end of the stitches on the back needle, and holding together two needles in parallel with an equal number of stitches on each, start by bringing the yarn through the first st on the front needle as if to purl, leaving the st on the needle. Take the yarn through the corresponding back st as if to knit, again leaving that st on the needle. *Bring the yarn back and through the same front st as already threaded, but this time as if to knit and slip this st off the needle. Next take the yarn through the next front st as if to purl, again leaving the st on the needle and then go to the first back st and bring the needle through as if to purl and slip that st off, then through the next back st as if to knit, leaving it on the needle.* Now repeat from * to * until all the stitches are used.

Decorations

To make **tassels**, wind yarn around a piece of card then cut along one edge to create even lengths. For the tea and cafetière cosies (see page 78) we used card 4 in (10 cm) wide; for the egg cosies 2 in (5 cm) wide. Take six lengths for small tassels and 20 for large ones, fold in half and tie yarn tightly around the center, leaving ends long enough to sew onto the item. Bend lengths back together and wind a piece of yarn around the bunch several times 0.5 in (1 cm) from tied fold.

To make **pom-poms**, cut out two discs of card, each with a central hole. For the tea and cafetière cosies (see page 78) we used a diameter of 4 in (10 cm) and a hole of 0.75 in (2 cm). For the egg cosies, a diameter of 2.5 in (6.5 cm) and a hole of 0.7 in (1.5 cm). For the beanies (see page 92) a diameter of 3 in (8 cm) and hole of 0.75 in (2 cm). Using a darning needle, and with the disks held together, wind a doubled length of yarn around them until they are well covered. Slip the point of a pair of scissors between the wool and discs and cut around the edge. Pull the discs slightly apart, leaving the ends caught, and wind yarn very tightly around threads between the discs and tie securely, leaving long ends. Slide off the discs.

Bibliography

This is a personal choice of a few books that have inspired, informed, and challenged me, and that focus on specific breeds and some knitting techniques and designs. I am an avid collector of knitting books, so this selection was difficult to make—some of the books may only be available secondhand, but I think they will be worth seeking out. I hope you find these books as interesting as I do!

BOOKS ABOUT SHEEP, SPINNING, FLEECE, AND FIBER

Robson, Deborah, and Ekarius, Carol, *The Fleece and Fiber Sourcebook* (Storey Publishing, 2011)

Fournier, Nola and Jane, *In Sheep's Clothing: A Handspinners Guide to Wool* (Interweave Press, 2003)

Jackson, Constance, and Plowman, Judith, *The Woolcraft Book: Spinning, Weaving, Dyeing* (Collins/Scribner, 1982)

British Wool Marketing Board, *British Sheep & Wool, A Guide to British Sheep Breeds and Their Unique Wool* (British Wool Marketing Board, 2010)

Jenkins, J. Geraint, *From Fleece to Fabric: The technological history of the Welsh Woolen Industry* (Gomer, 1981)

Davies, John William, *Welsh Sheep and Their Wool,* (Gomer, 1981)

Jenkins, J. Geraint, *Drefach and the Woolen Industry* (Gomer, 1981)

Teal, Peter, *Hand Woolcombing and Spinning, A Guide to Worsteds from the Spinning-Wheel* (Blandford Press, 1985)

Buchanan, Rita, *A Dyer's Garden* (Interweave Press, 1995)

BOOKS ABOUT KNITTING

Crompton, Claire, *The Knitter's Bible* (David & Charles, 2004)

Walker, Barbara G., *A Treasury of Knitting Patterns* (Schoolhouse Press, 1998) (See also pretty much anything by this great woman! This includes her second, third, and fourth books of knitting patterns, including charts, and also *Knitting from the Top.*)

Thomas, Mary, *Mary Thomas's Book of Knitting Patterns* (Dover, 1972)

Rutt, Richard, *A History of Handknitting* (Batsford, 1987) (Now out of print but also published by Interweave Press)

Zimmerman, Elizabeth, *Knitting without Tears* (Simon & Shuster, 1973)

Zimmerman, Elizabeth, *Knitter's Almanac* (Dover, 1982)

Foale, Marion, *Classic Knitwear* (Rodale Press, 1985)

Gibson, Priscilla A, and Robson, Deborah, *Knitting in the Old Way* (Nomad Press, 2004)

Wright, Mary, *Cornish Guernseys and Knit-frocks* (Alison Hodge/Ethnographica, 2008)

Kagan, Sasha, *Big and Little Sweaters* (Dorling Kindersley, 1987)

Starmore, Alice, *Aran Knitting* (Dover, 1999)

Starmore, Alice, *Fair Isle Knitting* (Taunton Press, 1993)

Starmore, Alice, *Fisherman's Sweaters* (Collins & Brown, 1994)

Interweave Press produces many useful books and among my favorites are *Folk Vests* by Cheryl Oberle, *Folk Socks* by Nancy Bush, and *Slip-stitch Knitting* by Roxana Bartlett. You will also find useful books on specific techniques or pieces (e.g. toys, tea-cosies, etc.) at Search Press and Schoolhouse Press.

KNITTING BLOGS

Knitter's Review by Clara Parkes. www.knittersreview.com
Needled by Kate Davies. http://textisles.com

RESOURCES

The internet is an excellent resource for knitters, whether you are looking for videos explaining how to cast on or yarn suppliers. Here are some tips on how to find Blacker Yarns as well as your local pure wool suppliers. Blacker Yarns were used for all the projects in this book. If you want to use other yarns—including ones you have spun yourself—you must adjust the tension and pattern as necessary. Our website features the additional designs featured in this book and more: www.blackeryarns.co.uk or contact me at info@blackeryarns.co.uk.

Pure wool and single-breed yarns are also made by companies including Rowan Yarns (www.knitrowan.com); Jamieson & Smith (www. shetlandwoolbrokers.co.uk); and R.E. Dickie (www. britishwool.com).

To find suppliers local to you, or yarn from a particular breed, search online for breed societies, farms or smallholdings, spinneries, farm shops, and agricultural, sheep or wool shows. Many farmers have blogs which will bring you closer to the farm and yarn producer.

The National Needlearts Association has a list of retailers www.tnna.org.

Creative Ewe knitting kits using Blacker Yarns www. blackerdesigns.co.uk

Ravelry A great place to meet likeminded knitters and research pure wool yarns. www.ravelry.com.

Index

Acknowledgements

Picture credits

We would like to thank the following for their kind permission to reproduce their photographs: **Alison Casserly** 38; **Amanda Crawford** 55; **Amanda Jones** 48; **British Wool Marketing Board** 6 bl, 12 bl, 15, 16 br, 20, 25, 32, 44, 46 br, 67, 75, 96, 101, 103, 109, 115, 131 br; **Diana Alderson** 80; **Diana Steriopolis** 14, 89; **Dominic Heneghen** 52, 54; **Douglas Bence** 7, 19 br, 112, 117 br; **iStock** 8 bl, br, 9 bl, 10 bl, 11 tr, 132, 134 bl, 138; **Jane Dansie** 123; **Jennie Martin** 49; **John Eveson** 9 br, 58; **Julie Halliday** 1, 39; **Karen Marshalsay** 127; **Linda Lunn** 79; **Myra Mortlock** 36; **Rita Taylor** 65; **Sam Morgan Moore** 2, 3, 4, 6 br, 8 background, 13 tl, 13tr, 16 c, 17, 18 background, bl, br, 19 bl, bc, 21 inset, 22, 23, 24, 26 inset, 27, 28, 30, 33 inset, 34, 35, 40 inset, 41, 42, 43, 45 inset, 46 bl, bc, 47, 49, 50, 51, 53 inset, 55, 57 59 inset, 60, 61, 62, 64, 65, 66, 68 inset, 69, 70, 72, 73, 76 inset, 77, 78, 79, 81 inset, 82, 83, 85, 86, 88, 90 inset, 91, 92, 97 inset, 98, 99, 102 inset, 10, 104, 110 inset, 111, 116 inset, 117 cr, 118, 119, 122, 124 inset, 125, 126, 130 background, bl, br, 131 bl, tr, 136; **Sarah Shourie** 72; **Sasha Kagan** 118; **Sian Brown** 126; **Simon Pask** 21, 26, 33, 40, 45, 53, 59,68, 76, 81, 90, 97, 102, 110, 116, 124; **Tina Barrett** 31, 131 bc; **Vampy** 56.
Abbreviations: bl bottom left, br bottom right, c center, tl top left. tr top right.

Author's acknowledgments

I would like to thank the everyone who has contributed to this book. The photographers Sam Morgan Moore, Douglas Bence, Diana Alderson, Diana Steriopolis, Dominic Heneghen, John Eveson, Simon Pask and Julie Halliday; models Andrea, Katie, James, Finley, Sam and Miles; all the designers and knitters; and the patient editor and designer Julie Brooke and Louise Turpin.

I have written this book by standing on the shoulders of giants, people such as Robert Bakewell, who created the modern Leicester breed and Jo Henson, who saved the Castlemilk Moorit from extinction. I have also consulted the work of specialist writers of much more detailed, informative and better researched books on wool and yarns, a selection of which are listed in the bibliography.

I owe a debt to my mother who loved wool cloth, and probably taught me to knit (I cannot actually remember learning to knit, although I remember learning to read and write) and who knitted all our pullovers; to my own Ambler ancestors, who by working in the worsted trade in Bradford led me to understand that running a wool mill is a possibility; to Barbara Willis and Jane Deane who taught me to spin, and to the many in the wool trade, particularly Bob Armitage, Richard Brown and Robert Hirst, who, despite their misgivings about a woman starting a wool mill in Cornwall, have been unfailingly supportive.

I must also thank my whole family and the many friends, but especially Douglas my husband and Sam our son, for putting up with the whole sheep and wool obsession, looking after the sheep, modelling the clothes, picking up the pieces, cooking the meals, and helping to drink the wine.